Norma's Journey

Stories and Prayers from Her Heart

Norma Sides

Cover design by Wendy Bawabe. Cover images include
the ship's manifest from USAT *Republic* which
left Shanghai on December 2, 1948, and arrived in
Seattle on December 22, 1948;
photo of Norma at Kiangwan Airfield, 1945;
photo of hand carved desk from Shanghai, 1947;
photo of Norma by Martha Dickinson, 2016;
paintings by Norma Sides.

Transcribed and edited by
Pamela Neilsen Johnson, Carolyn Auwers Tatarian, and Stephanie Johnson

DEDICATION

To Karen Harvey
and the choir from the bottom of my heart,
thank you for this choir experience and friendship.
It's one of the best things of my life.
I know I am surrounded by God's love and the choir members.
I really feel joyful. Life is good. I am blessed every day.

I just love music. It's an integral
part of my life every day.
Music makes me so aware of the thankfulness
in my heart to the choir members
who have driven me at night to choir practices.

Bonnie McKeon
Brad and Nancy Moses
Paul and Beth Haight

I also want to give deepest thanks to
Gail Nogueira for giving me constant
help and reassurance with my music.

So many members of the choir have always bolstered
my confidence by saying,
"We need your spirit and smile."
Thank you! Thank you!
You are a choir of God's angels here on earth.

In memory of my loving husband Bob
who taught me so much about how to live in America
and how thoughtfulness and kindness should
be a part of life every day.

Thank you to Pam Johnson and Carolyn Tatarian
who inspired me to move forward with
my life story and also with my prayers.
They did all the typing and corrections, gave me ideas,
and helped solidify some of my thoughts.
They shared their excitement,
touched my heart, and made this book a reality
with their precious time.
Words are not sufficient for their love and effort.
I am blessed.
Thank you for being my friends.
Thank you for being a treasure in my life.

CONTENTS

MY LIFE STORY

Shanghai, a Melting Pot

I was born on February 6, 1928, in Shanghai, China. Life was good. For most foreigners a well-paid job was the enticing element for living in Shanghai, drawing many nationalities from many countries to the "Pearl of the Orient." My father, like most others, felt the urge, the love of travel and one of moving forward, so he so decided to go to Shanghai. His first job was with the Holland China Trading Company Export and Import. Second, he became the attorney general for the Portuguese Consulate. He also had his own private successful law practice. In fact, he was one of the most sought after attorneys in the city of Shanghai. Here in this city, he met my mother and married her. Our home was at No. 9 Albury Lane.

The skyline of Shanghai resembled that of New York, London, or any large city. The British and French influenced much of the architecture of most of the buildings, hotels, banks, theatres. All were beautiful masterpieces of art—black marble, high rises, elevators, sculptures, gigantic lions at entrances to a bank, glass front boutiques, restaurants on ground floors of hotels and stores. There were traffic lights with an occasional policeman in a box at the center of some streets.

Shanghai, the sixth largest city in the world, had a population of about 3 million people in the 1930s. Shanghai was a melting pot, a haven, for many nationalities: a great atmosphere! Because of its cosmopolitan air, there was a variety of churches including Buddha temples, Jewish synagogues, Greek orthodox, Russian orthodox, Catholic, and Protestant. Going along with that, there were a variety of schools and universities. People of all nationalities came to Shanghai to live primarily for business, but also because it was a haven for refugees. Historically I don't think that many people were aware that at least two mammoth ships brought German Jews from Germany and parts of Europe to Shanghai as Hitler emerged as the leader in power. The same applied to a lot of white Russians who also settled in this city. Italians, Filipinos, Germans, and Indians settled here, too.

Class was stressed in China. The effects were prevalent in public conveyances and transportation: 1st class, 2nd class, 3rd class. In 3rd class the gate-like door on trains never had to be opened or closed. The people were so jammed in there they simply fell out. Class was stressed in theatres, too. Cheap seats were in the front. Middle seating was more expensive. The rear seats were a little less. The upper level loge seats were expensive, the rear cheaper. Class also was evident in clothing. The poor and labor class wore cotton. Middle class and wealthy wore silk and brocade.

In a funeral white is the color. The widow wears a white flower in her hair. Most hair dos were pulled back in a sleek manner in a bun at the nape of the neck. The smooth hair was attained by mixing wood shavings with a sticky solution in a mug. A toothbrush dipped into this sticky solution and then applied to the hair did the trick. A processional funeral parade goes to the Buddha temple where people place paper money and fruit.

Respect for family name and elders is stressed in the Chinese culture. Never bring shame to the family. Families choose a husband-to-be. Red is the color for the bride. The "Bride's Chair" is all covered up with curtains, and the trousseau, furniture, and dishes are loaded on trucks for display throughout the city.

2

One had to pay for one's education. Since class was stressed at that time, the poor rarely got to go to school; only the middle class and the wealthy. We all spoke several languages, including the Shanghai dialect because of our daily routine and life that brought us into contact with friends who spoke another language. Most of us understood or spoke five languages. However, the English language ruled supreme in all schools. We could select the school, but not the curriculum in two languages. We had L'Ecole Françoise, Jeanne D'Arc, St. Xavier's, Cathedral School for Girls, Aurora University, St. John's University Chinese School, Kaiser Wilhelm, Jewish, Cathedral, Thomas Hanbury, and an American school.

Shanghai, as a city, had four main boundaries.

International Settlement

French Town   Hongkew

Chinese City

There was the Hongkew district, the other side of the "Garden Bridge," and The International Settlement: the famous Bund and Broadway Mansions where the English and French architecture was seen and felt. Nanking Road and Bubbling Well Road are two streets I remember. The banks were gorgeous, made of marble, imposing two lions in front. Hotels and theatres were there, too. The Park Hotel across from the Race Course was famous for its ceiling that opened up on the 14th floor so that you could dance under the stars. We also had Chinese City where the streets were all named in Chinese. In French Town all the streets were named in French, such as Avenue de Roi Albert, Avenue Pòtain, Rue Lafayette, and Avenue Joffre. The airports were Kiangwan, Lunghwa, Hungao, and Zickawei Observatory.

The only huge piece of green within the city was the Race Course. There horse racing, lawn balls (bocce), tennis, soccer, swimming, bowling, and softball took place.

The Chinese Year

The Chinese Year is divided into four seasons. There are four animal symbols and four flower symbols. If your birthday falls in one of the winter months, you would be the {W} West wind, your flower would be the plum blossom, and your animal would be a tortoise. The winter symbol means long life, strength, and endurance.

Spring
{E} East Wind
Flower — peony (prosperity, love)
Animal — dragon (life's renewal)
Symbolic meaning — power, life's renewal

Summer
{S} South Wind
Flower — lotus (warmth, joy)
Animal — phoenix bird (serenity)
Symbolic meaning — peace, joy, and good luck

Autumn
{N} North Wind
Flower — chrysanthemum (nobility, elegance)
Animal — white tiger (courage)
Symbolic meaning — maturity, fulfillment

Winter
{W} West Wind
Flower — plum blossom (long life, beauty)
Animal — tortoise (longevity)
Symbolic meaning — long life, strength, and endurance

Chinese Symbols

Everything has a meaning. A Chinese ox or cow means good luck. The New Year is the biggest holiday. To this day oranges are an important symbol in China. You pay debts with a basket of oranges. They are also a cure for a cold. At Chinese New Year a basket of oranges as a gift is a good omen. At the New Year fuchsia and red envelopes with gold characters are used for gifts of money.

Odd numbers are good luck. Incense chases away the evil spirits. Jade brings good luck; so do a dragon and a peach stone. A willow branch over door equals good luck. A butterfly symbolizes happiness, and an azalea symbolizes womanhood. Bamboo symbolizes long life. A rice cake symbolizes a family circle with peace and harmony. A bamboo pole could be a clothesline. It was also used for carrying everything heavy. Chanting 'eh-oh-eh-ho' lightens the load. That's psychology again.

The Market Place

The market place was busy and full of activity. You'd see a half a pig and a cow hanging in the market place. You'd carry home live crabs, monkey brains, eels and quail eggs. You had to watch out for thieves.

Rice came in different qualities. The poor bought rice that had worms and husks in it. The better rice cost more. When you cook the rice, you put the amount you want into a pan. Then you add water to the height of the second line on your finger. The rice that burns on the bottom of the pan becomes your breakfast the next morning and is called "congee." You eat it with peanuts and salted fish. Black eggs were expensive. They are made by covering eggs with manure until the white becomes greenish-black and the yolk becomes a deep yellow. Black eggs are dipped in soy sauce, and they have a tangy taste.

Life Before the War

I lived in the Hongkew District on Albury Lane. We had a good-sized home with a huge living room downstairs that had wooden sliding panels dividing it. One half of the room was my father's law office. He had a huge safe and a gigantic glass-topped desk. The walls were filled with glass fronted book shelves. There was another room for Sho-long, and he had his own desk. Sho-long was the servant messenger boy who lived with us. His job was to run messages from our home to Dad's office at the Holland China Trading Company. His one request was to learn the English language, so Dad taught him. He was a happy, singing, whistling individual. Our other servant was Baby-Amah. She did the cooking and took care of us children, my two younger brothers and me. My older brother and sister were of age and were more independent.

Beyond Sho-long's room were the kitchen and a tiny bedroom off that for Baby-Amah. The kitchen had a silent butler that we kids could get into from my older brother's room and come down into the kitchen. Then we had a little back courtyard with a bathroom for the servants and a large black gate that was kept locked at all times. At the front, the main stairway led you upstairs to another small kitchenette, bathroom, and a huge bedroom with a verandah across the whole front of the house. I loved that verandah. The dining room and more sleeping quarters were also upstairs.

At the bottom of the main stairway all our names were put on a wooden sign with *in/out,* and we were taught that upon entering or leaving the home we had to slot the sign *in* or *out*. My father did this, too. He was a very busy man and this way we knew immediately if he was *in* or *out*. At the top of the main stairway was the telephone and that rang constantly.

One thing my father did every Saturday was to take time in the morning with us to give us our pocket money and ask if we had any needs. One time I needed some new shoes. He told me he would take me shopping alone, and then for waffles at a restaurant. He was gentle, a kind man. He had a brilliant mind. Actually he was Mom and Dad to us. We walked everywhere—to school, church, and catechism. We walked to everything and thought nothing of it.

School Years

I started kindergarten at five years (English influence) in an English school Thomas Hanbury. It was within walking distance, crossing two main roads. Baby-Amah took my two young brothers and me to the park every afternoon where I played in the sand or on the swings. It was a great neighborhood, Albury Lane.

Pierce Apartments was a huge high rise. What was different about the high rises was that the street level was always made into boutiques and bake shops for the public access, not just within a hotel or an apartment. Tchakalian Brothers had lollipops that were to die for—yummy, sticky caramel.

Club Lusitano was on the top floor of the Pierce Apartments. Every Sunday my godmother would take me to church, then we'd go there for lunch and my special drink "strawberry melba" that I drank while she played cards or mah-jong for a while. She also took me overnight, and holidays always brought something special from her. My largest Easter gift was from her. I'll never forget it. It was a little village with a huge tree trunk of milk chocolate and bunnies and candies. Wow! My godmother was extraordinary. She devoted her whole life to caring for her sister who was born deformed with a hunchback and a nephew whose mother didn't have time for him. She never married.

At seven I started dancing school—tap, ballet, and ballroom— twice a week at the Lyceum Theatre in French Town. I was good at it, appearing on stage. I went to catechism class on Saturday mornings. I made my first communion at Sacred Heart Church in the Hongkew district. It was a huge church right across from St. Xavier's School for boys.

As I grew and moved on in school, I made the upper school transition from I to II, et cetera. After homework we kids would go outdoors and play "Kick-the-Can" or "Hide 'n' Go-Seek" with both girls and boys. Lots of kids from Pierce Apartments would join in, the English Watson's and an American family the Beeman's. Boy, those boys were handsome and their sister was pretty. We'd also ride the elevator at Pierce Apartments all the way to the top and play on the roof garden. I thought the Pierce Apartments were super. They were built like a huge brick and marble block with verandahs. Inside was a huge compound with back entrances to everyone's kitchen for deliveries. Life was good. I was nine years old. The year was 1937. Now in the evenings there was a lot of talk and rumors about a war, about a Japanese invasion.

War Breaks Out: The Beginning of My Faith Journey

It was August 1937. On Albury Lane, there was one Japanese family. They thought that if the attack came, and the war started, it would not hit our Hongkew district first. Everyone was getting concerned, and the number one topic of each day would be about

8

a Japanese invasion; however, everyone continued on, living day to day.

One night I played "Kick the Can" and "Hide 'n' Seek" with the neighbor kids and some from the high rise Pierce Apartments. All week talk was of the war but no one knew where the attack was going to be.

The next morning my mother said to me that my two wealthy aunts were getting nervous about the war, and that they were moving away from the Hongkew district. They purchased a house in the French sector and felt they would be safer there. They asked my mother to help them move. This particular morning, Baby-Amah had gone to the market place. Mum told me she was going to leave for Aunties' house and the phone number was by the telephone, 7776. One servant named Sho-long was home with my two baby brothers and me, and Baby-Amah would be home shortly from the market.

All of a sudden all hell broke loose. Explosions and gun fire began. Noise came from the streets and people were running everywhere, trampling and pushing hundreds of people. My brothers were crying. I ran to the verandah, and my neighbor was shouting that I had to leave now and go with her. She was yelling that I had to throw together a change of clothes, gather up my brothers, and leave with her immediately, or else the bridge would be blockaded and we would be stuck there. I said, "I have to think about it."

I ran in and fell on my knees and prayed to God. I ran back to the verandah and told my neighbor, "I'm not going." I ran back in and wrapped my two brothers in blankets, and the three of us hid under the bed. I tried to comfort my brothers. I knew someone would come to get us.

Shrapnel were flying. I looked from the verandah towards Pierce Apartments and saw a man who was taking in his canary from his verandah. He got hit and fell to the ground. I was scared. The streets were full of people panic stricken, yelling and screaming. Sho-long said that he was sorry, but he was running away, too. My two baby brothers were crying and yelling, too. I was alone with the two of them.

I remember kneeling and praying, asking God to help me. Looking back, I know this was the start of my journey of faith, my spiritual journey. I ran to the verandah again and told my neighbor across the street I was going to remain, because I knew Mum and Baby-Amah would be trying to get home to us. I then called my aunts' home, and they said Mum was on her way home.

My oldest brother who had joined the volunteer corps had his uniform on and was called out, so I knew he would be heading home to save us. My journey of faith continued. Just a feeling of God telling me I made the right decision helped me. I knew I had done the right thing by staying put because Mum and Lulu, my older brother, reassured me of it. True enough, Baby-Amah and Mum made it home. Then my older brother appeared in uniform and said, "There is no time to waste. Grab a toothbrush and a change of clothes and follow me."

Lulu told us not to open our mouths, simply bow our heads to the Japanese soldiers who were already barricading the bridge. He would try to get us through. I was scared silly. We got to the bridge, and there were soldiers with fixed bayonets poking them into bundles and bags. My brother spoke to them. We bowed. He told them that my dad's export and import office was just down the street and would they please allow us to go there. They let us through the barbed wire. Phew!

Simultaneously 23 warships and flagship "Izumo" were in the Whangpoo River shelling us. By the time we got through there were ten miles of refugees trying to cross the bridges. So many were killed by the fixed bayonets. Babies were thrown into garbage cans, truckloads of dead piled high were dumped in empty spots and burned.

We made it to Dad's office. We were so relieved to see him. Even though we had just lost our home and all our belongings, we had each other. We slept on the floor on cardboard and papers. The next day amongst the chaos Dad found us an apartment on Bubbling Well Road in the International Settlement. Here started a new chapter in my life. Baby-Amah was still with us. She was getting older and thinking of going home to her family as soon as we found a new servant to take her place.

Life During the War

During this time I lived hungry with no power, no water, and no stores. There were curfews because of rape, blockages constantly, and searches with fixed bayonets into the mattresses. A spy was sent into our apartment to check on us constantly as my father was in the Portuguese Embassy. The Bridge House, a huge apartment complex, was the torture house. You never came out alive. The Japanese anti-aircraft were on the top of large apartment buildings. All the firing killed innocent people, but they never reached the American planes.

The Japanese confiscated our school in the Hongkew district, so for a while our education was interrupted. I went to a huge school the public Thomas Hanbury School for girls for a while. The Japanese said we could use the German school Kaiser Wilhelm Schule on Great Western Road, part of the day. We all

11

went there, but it was not a good solution. When the boarding school where I lived was on Tifeng, we walked to school on Jessfield Road. We walked from the boarding school on Great Western to school on Tifeng Road. The next change was to move our school to some old sheds on Tifeng Road. None of the schools were co-educational except for the American school. Now these sheds we girls had to go to were right beside the boys' school, and every time we had gym or a hockey game, they would laugh and make fun of us. I was shy and appalled by this.

Dad was now the attorney for the Portuguese Embassy. Swimming lessons started for me at the "Y," a nine a.m. class. The "Y" was also across the Race Course, right beside the Park Hotel. One of the best treats was to have a "pony express" sundae (like a banana split here), the coffee shop's specialty. One wall was mirrored behind the soda fountain counter, and the other whole wall was plate glass, so you could eat and watch the people go by.

Life Gets Tougher

Thank goodness our schooling was done before the war got worse. The Japanese got tough. They interned all Americans and British. The Americans were bombing us strategically. We had some water but no power. We had to fill our bath tub with water early in the morning, and that water had to last all day for food, washing, and flushing the basin. Everything had to be boiled. We used charcoal to cook with and to fill the irons. Some even ran cars with charcoal.

We woke up one morning, and most stores had been boarded up. Food was hard to come by. The thieves were waiting for you at the main market place on Seymour Road. If you returned home with what you bought, you were lucky!! The thieves were quick and adept at cutting holes in your bag and running away. They killed dogs and cats and filled the dumplings chaos-sei-pao with that ground up meat. People got sick.

Every foreigner was rationed one half pound of bread per day. We had large teapots. Leaves were put in and you'd walk to the hot water store and buy your hot water to fill your teapot and thermos. It was a luxury. One not only bought your hot water there, it was also the restaurant for all rickshaw coolies. They survived on uzakwei, a fried twisted pastry inserted into a ball of steamed rice. They also ate baked sweet potatoes. The rickshaw coolie would pull his rickshaw to the side walk, set it down, get his food and tea, and then be ready to haggle his next fare.

If one wanted hot bath water, two wooden buckets were delivered to your place. Providing you didn't live in a high rise, or too far a distance, the water would arrive fairly warm and not half spilled out.

Cholera was prevalent. People were dying. Shanghai was cut off from everything. The harbor was blockaded. There was not much food, water, or medicine. We all got very hungry. There were days when I knelt and prayed for long periods of time to ease my hunger pains. God already had touched me. My journey of faith continued. I felt God's touch in my life. The Black Market mushroomed. Sugar would be wet, so it would weigh more. So the one half pound of bread we stood in line for was heavier, it got filled with stones and dead worms from the bad flour.

Chinese Medicine

Chinese medicine stores are unique. If one has a stomach ache you tell the man your ailments. He will put dried mold, bugs, grasshoppers, and rat's ears on a piece of paper made out of

13

pressed manure, and fold it very carefully and securely into a triangle because it resembles the bound feet of Chinese women. You go home, add water to the dried things, boil it, and one drink cures you. It works. I've tried it.

The other medicine they use involves dipping a copper coin into a little dish of peanut oil and then scraping the skin the length of the throat until blood almost comes through the outer layer of skin. If that person had sickness below the neck, the scraping of the skin would be done across the top of the rib cage and the back by one's shoulder blades.

Every day of my life, people walked by me with these visible stripes, and it wasn't until I became older did I realize the meaning of it all. Psychology: that's what it was. The scraping was so painful, you'd forget about whatever else was bothering you!! Another cure required putting some black ointment on rice paper which was then heated and then applied to a swollen area. To ease achy feet, one soaked their feet in a basin of hot water that had orange skins and dried boiled pomelo skins in it. And along with this, rock candy put into a pear and baked would do wonders.

During the war, it was not safe to be out on the streets after four in the afternoon. If you were, chances were you'd be raped, robbed, or killed. It was blackout every night. If a light beam was seen, you would be in big trouble. The light we had was made by filling a glass with water and peanut oil, and then adding a wick. We had no power and no radios and at any given time, the Japanese gendarme would knock, enter, and go through mattresses and wardrobes poking bayonets. Another day the Japanese soldiers came and ripped radiators out of the wall from everyone's house or apartment. They needed metal for bullets. It left such a mess with holes in the walls.

We knew the war must be going against them. They were using desperate measures. One day they decided to dig up the sidewalks every 200 yards for machine gun dug outs as a last stand. We had no power for years so it was pitch black out there. With no power people who were out fell in and broke their legs. Babies were thrown in to die. We continued to use peanut oil and water in a glass and had little wicks floating in it for light.

The Japanese also thought putting dynamite on the 2nd or 3rd floor of any high rise apartment or hotel would be a good idea should the Americans bomb again. That way, city people would be hurt, too!! When my uncle came, he always treated me to a baked sweet potato. That was my meal. I still love sweet potatoes!!

I saw American planes all the time. One B-29 flew so low you could see the pilot! Air raid sirens were blowing constantly. The Japanese wouldn't engage in too many dog fights, instead anti-aircraft guns killed more innocent people with shrapnel, et cetera because when the air raid siren sounded, barbed wire barricades would shoot across the main streets and trap the people there. There were no air raid shelters. It was a no-win situation.

We endured nine long years of this chapter. My brother Eddie (Sonny) came down with cholera and almost died. I was food poisoned. We survived.

My older sister, Noemi, six years my senior, was an excellent secretary. She worked at the Embassy with my father, and was secretary to the Consul General. She was presented to society at 21, was always on the Ten Best Dressed list, and was star short stop on the softball team for Club Lusitano. She owned her own bike, a two-tone green and chrome job. She was amazing in all

15

her endeavors—champion soft ball team, quick runner, tennis, ballet.

I remember when she got a case of strawberry jam, and she locked it up in her wardrobe. We never got a taste of it, and we were so hungry. Because she was earning a salary she didn't have to wash clothes on an old wooden scrub board, iron, or sweep or clean. She got a bed to sleep in during the war. My brothers and I had to sleep on the floor. I did all the cleaning! My mother called me "Cinderella."

The War Ends

Once again rumors were flying. The Japanese will be leaving. They've lost the war. The Americans are coming. Could this be true? 1945, yes it was!! What a mess to clean up. Slowly, but surely, things began to improve.

In 1945, Americans freed us. I'm blessed. That war changed my life. Unbelievable, the war was over. The harbor opened and planeloads of Americans began to arrive. Flying over the hump to Shanghai were the 10th Air Force, 1439th AACS, Navy, and the Flying Tigers. They took over the Kiangwan Airfield. They also took over some huge apartment buildings like the Medhurst, Broadway Mansions, and New Asia Hotel for Americans and their families. Stores opened, the PX and the commissary. There were glorious foods of every kind. I remember a restaurant The Sun-Ya, a chocolate shop Bianchi's, and the bake shops New Kiessling Cafe and Kraft Bake Shop.

All Americans and British were released from internment camps to start life again.

Life After the War

Growing up I always stayed home caring for my two younger brothers, Mario and Sonny, and doing chores. Consequently, growing up during the war, I never really had any teen life to speak of. I really didn't date until 16 years of age. I also discovered I could sing. My first attempt was a talent show on radio station XMHC with three other girls. We sang harmony. We were good. Julie de Souza, Helen Britto, Camille Gutierez, and we called ourselves the "Young Ladies." From radio station singing, I branched out and sang solo. Bill Hagman, an American and Hennie Paulson, a Danish man, were our accompanists on piano.

The US Army was having tryouts for a singer with their band at the "Y." We were entertaining the troops with a show. I got the job. So, wherever the US Army band played, at the Capitol Theatre or an air base, I went around to sing. I also applied for a job as a telephone operator with the US Air Force. I got that job with the 10th Air Force. Now I had two jobs. I worked all day, and I sang at night. Needless to say, I got thin.

After the US Army band left, I sang at the Enlisted Men's Club some evenings, broadcast on the radio for ½ hour shows, and cut my first record. I also dated heavily. I couldn't believe that guys were chasing me for a change instead of my sister. Could be I was thinner, too.

I Meet Bob

As the various American outfits pulled out to go home, communications were moved to Shad Headquarters, a few miles out of Kiangwan Airfield. It was there that I met Bob. I wasn't overly taken with him at our first meeting. The weather station and control tower at Kiangwan Airfield were above each other at base operations. Bob was a control tower operator.

After our introduction by Mickey, the weather station sergeant, Bob called every day. He was having problems with his girl at home. She was dating, and he was pretty upset. So we talked for two to three months. He was so bummed out about his girl back home, he had stopped writing home. So I got him to write home again. His girl got pregnant and got married. So we went on our first date.

We went to supper in French Town to "The Balalaika," a Russian restaurant. We danced and had a great time. He began to grow on me. He had some great qualities—dependable, thoughtful, and loving. After a year, he proposed. I accepted. We went shopping for a small diamond, started a hope chest, and bought a carved camphor chest. Back home, however, his father was a very sick man with leukemia at Massachusetts Memorial General Boston.

As both of us were underage (not 18) we had to wait for his parental permission. Meantime the CID (Criminal Investigation Department) investigated my family, and I was given a thorough medical exam. Bob's mother was having a difficult time accepting the fact her son wanted to marry a foreigner. So she continued to stall the permission. As I look back now, this should have been a major sign to me of trouble, but Bob kept reassuring me that after she met me, she would love me. Things got worse: she disliked Catholics. I was one. She disliked colored people. I was from another country with an olive complexion. She even wanted to know what my blood consisted of. I had to reply by letter my father was Portuguese and Spanish, and Mum was French, German, and Chinese—five nationalities. Bob's whole family had to meet and vote on this "permission of our marriage." One sister Mildred and her husband Alan Litchfield were on our side, so with that, we got our letter. Phew!!

By then I was getting upset and angry. Coming from a prominent well-known family within a huge city, I was insulted. I had never had to deal with such an issue. In Shanghai all races and religions lived in harmony. I finally told Bob when his tour of duty was up to go home, and I would join him stateside later. He left, against his will, for Japan where a ship would take him home from the Repo Depot outside of Yokohama.

Bob Returns!

After he left, I started to do some deep thinking and decided the heck with his mother. I did want to marry him. Alas, he was in Japan. How was I going to reach him? First thing in the morning I called my girlfriend who was secretary to the colonel at Shad Headquarters and asked her for an appointment with the colonel. He saw me that afternoon, and I told him the whole story. He listened, looked at me, and said, "Norma, why didn't you marry him when he was here?" So I told him the more personal issues, including the fact that we had done our homework inquiring about all the data at the American Embassy and that marrying in Shanghai would be the best route to go. The colonel smiled and said that because he knew me, he would do all he could to help me. He was so nice to me. From that moment on things got unbelievable. Fate was on my side. The word was out! "Get ahold of Sgt. Sides 11077022 at Repo Depot!"

The Asian American Community Services (AACS) message center sent messages on the teletypes. Every pilot who flew to Tokyo took a message. All the ham operators sent messages. Gossip at the airbase and at headquarters was, "Who is this civilian Norma that the whole American Air Force is working

19

for?" The effort was fantastic. Pilots and ham operators checked in with me daily. The newspaper *Stars and Stripes* even heard about our story and wanted to interview us.

After a few days, success came. Bob phoned. He never got on that ship to go to the USA. Instead, he reenlisted and flew back to Shanghai. The US Air Force will always be special to me. They worked a miracle. I was ecstatic to have Bob back. Needless to say his mom was not pleased.

Bob and I Marry

We married on November 29, 1947, at Christ the King Church on Rue Bourgeat in French Town. My sister had married in May to an American Navy officer, and I was her maid of honor. They lived at the Cathay Mansions, a stone's throw from the church. So like any bride anywhere, I had my hair done at the salon, then went to my sister's for my bath and to get dressed for my wedding day. The Air Force even loaned us a staff car and driver for the day. That was terrific. It was a small wedding compared to my sister's big splurge of 200 at the Officer's Club, but we were happy with it all. Our reception was at the New Royal Hotel, and our honeymoon suite was at the Park Hotel.

Bob and I found a rental room, sharing the bathroom with a white Russian family, at the Majestic Apartments. We lived there until Bob got promoted to staff sergeant. Then the Air Force provided us with a lovely two room apartment and bath at the New Asia Hotel.

Our First Child

After being married a month, I learned I was pregnant so Bob's promotion was really timely. We were in our new provided

20

apartment before the arrival of the baby. On September 15, 1948, Dickie was born. The delivery was natural and quite easy. I did have to have a sniff of ether for one outer stitch.

The next day, however, Colonel Caples who delivered Dickie came in and told us that he was born with an enlarged thymus gland, which was impeding his breathing and turning him blue. So Colonel Caples arranged to have his thymus gland shrunk by three radium treatments at a French hospital in French Town since the Army hospital did not have the necessary equipment.

After each treatment, x-rays were taken. Colonel Caples also arranged for a staff car to drive Bob, me, and the baby. He was very thoughtful. I had to wear a protective apron whilst I held Dickie for his treatments. After the third treatment, Colonel Caples was satisfied with the shrinkage, breathing, and color, and I could go home with the baby. He was a good baby. Little did I know that this was the start of another whole chapter in our life.

Living at the New Asia Hotel with all the married NCOs and officers and wives was great. The food was excellent. After being without food for so long, I was in awe at the delicious meals attractively presented each and every day at the dining room of the New Asia Hotel. There were fresh flower stalls on the sidewalk by the entrance. I had fresh flowers in the apartment every day. Movies were provided on the 7th or 8th floor. The Army bus stopped at eight at the door so you could ride to Broadway Mansions then walk to the PX or commissary. America took good care of their personnel and families. I felt very special as I was a part of that.

Things were going too smoothly. There began an undertone of talk about Communism seeping into Shanghai. It got stronger. Chiang-Kai-Shek had fled to Formosa. Where did that good feeling of Americans being welcome go? Mobs stoned our busses shouting, "Mei-Kwo-Nying." (Americans go home.) It became serious. America ordered all dependents and children to leave immediately for the USA. After that all Army, Navy, and Air Force personnel had to leave, too.

Heading to America

Where I had just delivered a baby, Bob got to stay and leave for the States with me. It was the last ship for dependents, *The Republic*. It was huge. There were no more American ships after December 2, 1948.

It was an odd feeling, leaving behind a culture I'd known all my life. It was hard to say goodbye to my family. I had to believe I would see them sometime in the future. I know I felt numb and just went through the motions.

We left Shanghai, docked in Yokohama, Japan for a day or so, and then to Seattle, Washington instead of New York. There was a change in plans because of a typhoon. In Yokohama we picked up many GIs who had married Japanese girls. Also on board were all the missionaries who had been serving in the interior parts of China. We hit one typhoon during the three weeks on board. That was scary. I thought I might never see land again.

I was thrilled to see Mt. Rainier and Puget Sound as the ship docked. It was beautiful! Seattle looked like a Christmas tree with homes nestled in the hills and lit up and covered with snow. Yes, it was almost Christmas Day.

Now started the fun of immigration. It went on and on. Finally, the officials got down the alphabet to "S" (Sides), and as I took my turn the immigration men kissed me. They couldn't believe I spoke English. Most of the Japanese wives we added to the passenger list spoke very little English. Poor men had a trying day! All cleared, next stop was an Army bus to transport us to the base, Fort Lewis, to live until Bob got discharged from the service. From there we flew to Boston where Bob's sister and husband (the Litchfield's) met us and took us to their home on Newton Avenue in Braintree. That night all of Bob's family arrived to meet me. Coming from a family of nine, I thought there was no end to these Sides.

Life in Hanover

We continued to live in Braintree as Bob's father was very ill with leukemia at Massachusetts Memorial in Boston. He was a police officer in Boston and took sick one year or so prior to retirement. He had an apartment in Boston plus the home on Main Street in Hanover.

After a day's rest, the Litchfield's thought Bob and I should go to the hospital and meet Mom and Dad Sides. Upon arrival there, I was told by the nurses that Dad Sides was staying alive to meet me and that he wanted to be strong enough to walk to the elevator to greet me. He did that! I felt he welcomed me, not so with Mom Sides. My perception would prove correct shortly.

Upon reflection Mom Sides and I got off to a bad start. First, the episode regarding the permission. Second, Bob's re-enlisting in the service just to marry me. Third, the mere act of me being a foreigner and Catholic. Some of these rigid stigmas were deeply entrenched.

After being home about a month, Bob's father died. Everyone in the family felt that Bob and I and the baby should live in the home in Hanover with his mom now that she was a widow. Bob was the only one without a home or an apartment of his own, so he was the logical one. Mom Sides got rid of the apartment in Boston, and we all began life once again together.

My first impression of Hanover was "Wow! This is it!" Cornfields across the street as far as the eye could see. There was a chicken farm and there were Great Danes beside the house. There were no stores at all but one general store, Brook's, and the Post Office. There were just houses. I was petrified of the Great Danes. The chicken houses smelled and attracted flies. The couple who owned the farm were great people, however. Alma King (the wife) always came over with eggs and conversation.

My highlight of the day was to go for a walk pushing the baby in the carriage to Brooks General Store. Brooks Store and Post Office was the meeting place for many in a small town. It was where you went for your mail, plus various food needs. There were a few cats always sleeping around on the bananas. It was very country quaint. Brooks Store was owned by Bob's oldest sister and husband John Brooks. He was also the post master. I'll never forget the day I asked if they had bananas to sell. The whole store went into a deep silence when I posed that question, and two or three people said quite loudly, "Did you hear her? She said 'bananas.'" Their interpretation of a foreigner was that you couldn't speak English. Fooled them!

Gradually I began to know people. They too were amazed I spoke good English. I was like a foreign apparition for these parts. People stared at me. Some would ask me if I was from Hawaii or the Philippines. After a while, whatever country they thought I was from, I would just smile and agree. Because to get into my mixed heritage of Portuguese, Spanish, German, French, Chinese was too much for them to comprehend.

24

Bob found a job at Hunt's Potato Chip Company in Braintree as a salesman. I became involved with church groups and Community Visiting Nurses and made friends so that afternoons were taken up with walks with other mothers and children.

Our New Roof!

Around this time the roof of the house needed shingling. Bob warned me that workmen would be arriving early, setting up the staging, et cetera. He told me to get dressed early. I did and when I ran outdoors to put the baby Mike into the carriage for his nap, my slip fell down in the driveway. I dressed so quickly that I never put the straps onto my shoulders. I was so embarrassed. The workmen just looked and laughed.

If that wasn't enough, in a while, one of the workmen knocked on the door. Upon answering it, he held a black roof shingle in his hand and asked me if I could get a cookie sheet and simply toast the shingle very quickly so that they could work easier. It was cold out there! I must have looked dumb founded, but I toasted those shingles for the workmen all day long.

In those days we had an old black iron stove with two burners. It was run by a tank of oil. The living/dining room had a space heater also run by oil. The bedrooms upstairs and the bathroom had no heat whatsoever. When we went to bed, I got dressed with layers of clothing, socks and all! Bob would say to me, "Are you coming or going?" I was always frozen. The bathroom was another trip into the frigid zone. I was so thin, I'd fall into the water, and at 40° that was an eye opener!

I never saw snow till I got here, and then all I did was shovel and hang clothes on a line that turned into frozen blobs

25

instantaneously. I was not wild about this northern tundra, but I didn't complain. Just put on more clothes and gloves!

Dickie's Test Results and Mike Is Born

Dickie the baby turned two and still couldn't walk. He was chubby and happy, period. The family doctor Dr. Peckham told me that he wanted Dickie to be taken into Children's Hospital in Boston for tests. I think now he had his suspicions about Dickie's progress. Bob took the day off, and into Boston we went. We spent the whole day there, going from one floor to another for tests from GI series to x-ray to neurology, et cetera—from head to toe. Finally when all was done, we were exhausted. Good thing we packed enough baby food and formula and diapers. The results would be forthcoming.

At this time I was about to have our second child and on March 7th our second son was born. Dickie's checkup and results were due at Children's. Bob went into Children's Hospital with Dickie, and I stayed home with Mike. The doctor there told Bob that Dickie was severely mentally retarded. The tests showed that in my third month of pregnancy, the whole process stopped, and instead of aborting, it started up again leaving this unborn child with many undeveloped areas.

The doctors suggested signing a paper to put him into an institution. We were devastated. It was the first time I saw my husband cry. Seeing Bob cry made me realize I had to be strong through this crisis. After much thought we decided to keep Dickie at home. I felt and was determined I could take care of him and the new baby, too. And I did.

Bob fenced in an area and built a sandbox, and the boys played and grew. We had a great family doctor, Dr. Donnelly in

26

Rockland. Mike our second child and son was born totally normal. That was my first question to Dr. Donnelly after the birth, "Is he all right?"

Because our first born was retarded, I think Bob and I tried so hard to be good parents. Mike was handsome, intelligent, and a super jock. We supported him in his every endeavor, and attended all his games. He was a three-letter jock—football, track, basketball. He was good, no question about it. He held the record for touchdowns on the South Shore. He ran a 440 super, and excelled academically with pushes from me. He did well enough to be inducted into the National Honor Society.

Our Family Grows: Judi and Susie

When Mike was 3, I gave birth again in 1955 to Judi our first girl. She was adorable. Both boys waited on her. She had a habit of always rubbing one shoe or sock off sitting in her baby butler, dropping her toys, and they just kept picking them up. She truly was the princess!! Our first girl, the apple of Bob's eye. Everywhere we went people noticed her. As Judi grew, she had a built-in family of friends, as our neighbor the Mesheaus had five daughters and one son. One of their daughters Ginny was Judi's age, so they became good friends, starting school together and playing together every day. In class and in Sunday school was another girl Lynne Johnson who lived on Walnut Street. They were very good friends. Judi's two brothers and she were very harmonious from the start, and that bonding is still there today in their adult life.

I then had Susie four years later. Although she was the fourth child, healthwise it was my hardest pregnancy. Phlebitis was painful and dogged me. Delivery took one and a half days. I passed a major blood clot a day or so later. The doctor told me I shouldn't have any more children; it was getting too risky.

Susie was the best baby. She was so good natured, and she loved to eat all the time. I couldn't wait for her to wake up from her nap, so we could enjoy each other. At six weeks she came down with pneumonia. Bob and I rushed her to the hospital as she wasn't breathing right. The doctors and nurses worked hard and pulled her through. That was scary. Once again I turned to God and prayed to save this baby. My prayers were answered.

At one year old, she came down with pneumonitis and had to stay at South Shore Hospital again. It was difficult seeing her and leaving her for all concerned. On the day she was going to come home Dr. Donelley called to say she had caught rubella measles so she would stay another day or two. What a tough beginning of life, but she made it. That special bonding and love between us remains today.

As Susie grew, she developed allergies on the palms and soles of her feet. We saw a dermatologist often. She suffered as the skin would crack and bleed. She couldn't participate in school gym because of it. She developed a love for horses. So Bob built a corral, moved the shed to the back of the yard, and turned it into a horse barn and hay loft. Susie rode "western" and won quite a few ribbons. We all went to the horse shows to cheer her on. First she had Tangerine, then Tonka, and third Cleopatra—three different horses. Tangerine had to be put to sleep. Tonka was sold because he was too frisky. Cleopatra was sold because it was getting too expensive to keep her, plus Susan was getting married. At one point our family had a horse, a golden retriever named Cheba, Zap the cat, and Daisy the guinea pig.

Cheba was family, but he was also Bob's best friend. Bob was a volunteer fireman in Hanover. Cheba rode to every fire with Bob and he also rode with Bob to work at the Water Department. Cheba always sat in the front seat with Bob. Always. So when I rode with Bob to go to the dump or anywhere else, I had to sit in the back seat. I sat in the front seat once and Bob told me that Cheba was upset and that I needed to move to the back seat because Cheba liked being with his stones and tennis balls on the floor in the front. I didn't mind at all. So, after I lost Bob, I just automatically went to the back seat in anyone's car! Choir members who drove me at night to choir rehearsal don't know this story which explains why I'm an automatic back seat person, no pun intended!

Dickie's Schooling

Around this time our retarded son was going to St. Coletta's as a day pupil. With the help of our Police Chief John Stoddard, he got enrolled. However, after being there for several years Sister Mary-George requested a meeting with me. It was nearing the end of school before summer vacation. The minute I received that letter, I knew in my heart what it would say. I went to my appointment with Sister Mary-George nervous and apprehensive because the bottom line was a deep perceptive feeling of bad news. It was. Sister Mary-George said that she felt they couldn't have Dickie as a student anymore because he was so severely handicapped.

If he could only do something with his hands, just something, they would consider his staying. The list of students from all over the USA was long, and it wasn't fair to them or to Dickie. He wasn't trainable. His attention span was zero. Behavioral problems were major. Well, I came home with a heavy heart. In those days a town had to have five retarded children before any help would be forthcoming. Hanover did not have that number. The problem was ours to have and to solve.

I had two and a half months before school started again to figure out my problem of Dickie. The first thing I did was to make a promise to myself that I would pray to God every single day for His help. I really needed it—marriage, a different country, a handicapped son, plus a mother-in-law who lived with me and didn't like me. In fact, she tried to make my life miserable. So my journey of faith continued. I prayed every day.

Poor Mike acted like the #1 son. I realize now that I always asked him to watch over Dickie. I put pressure on him unfairly. I know he resented Dickie following him around so much because Dickie would sometimes embarrass him when they'd be playing at a neighbor's yard. Mike would be thrown out of the yard because of Dickie. It was nothing for Dick to wear 14 different pairs of pants a day. His muscles were so underdeveloped that he had to wear special boots with metal plates around the ankle to support his stance. His male organs were underdeveloped, also his ribs.

My mother-in-law had chosen Judi for her pet. She felt bad for Dickie my retarded son, tolerated Susie, and disliked Mike. For years as the children grew, I cooked and served her and them and never got to sit down to a meal with them. It was just as well. She never made me feel welcome.

This was a summer I would never forget. Emergency runs to the hospital with Dickie. He'd severed a major vein in the yard with a piece of glass and did not know it. He went into a pond and got stuck on the muddy bottom with his head sticking out. All the while I changed Susie the baby. Checkup time was due for Susie, and Dr. Donnelley who made house calls also sat me down and really talked to me about Dickie. Even though I didn't want to hear all that was being said, he was right. I did have three other children to care for. Dickie required so much. He also advised me on some future problems.

I continued to pray. Bob worked so many hard, long hours at Hunt Potato Chip Company. He started out as a delivery man, was promoted to sales manager, and then was promoted to plant supervisor. He didn't see much of the children like most fathers in that era. They worked hard. Mothers stayed home and took care of the family.

My Prayers Are Answered!

I was a neat person who cleaned house every day. This day started out as any other morning. I prayed and started to house clean. As I cleaned, I felt my prayers were answered after over a month and a half of praying. I was told to telephone my selectman at Town Hall and tell him my predicament about my retarded son. I know it sounds crazy, this foreigner in a little town like Hanover who didn't even know Selectman Allan Carnes. I stopped cleaning. I got on the phone and called Mr. Allan Carnes. I told him my story: I had this retarded son who could not continue at St. Coletta's anymore. Come September he needed friends like any normal child, and I needed help to get him into the Paul Dever State School in Taunton. He listened to me and without hesitation said, "I'll go into the State House in Boston and see what I can do. I'll get back to you." This was a "Kairos" moment, as the Greeks would say, in my life.

When one feels God working in one's life, it's a wonderful warm feeling. A stranger in a new country feeling connected because of God. If you talked about it, most people would think you were crazy, but I felt it and lived through it. It really happens!! That peace was in my heart.

When Bob got home from work, I told him what I had done. He was shocked!! He had an idea by now that I didn't give up easily on problems. Shortly thereafter, true to his word, Mr. Carnes contacted our State Representative of Duxbury, a Mr. Francis Perry. He in turn wrote to me and before long we knew our son would be able to go to Paul Dever School. If that wasn't enough, they also worked out a more suitable financial fee for us. So many doors opened for us. I know it was because of God's answer to my prayer. So I started a busy time getting his clothes ready with name tapes, et cetera. Finally the day arrived. It was another soul wrenching day for us. Have you ever felt sad and heavy hearted even though you knew that what you're doing was the best and right thing? We said good bye, cried, and then drove home.

Home Life

My mother-in-law persisted in her meanness. One day she had a heart attack, and after hospitalization she came home. I waited on her with meals and bed pans till she recuperated. She thought it best that Bob buy the house from her as her health was jeopardized by her heart. She called a lawyer and had us sign a paper that we simply purchased the home at bank value, that her room would always be hers, and that all her possessions would also be hers. We did just that.

I was to clean the whole house, cook, wash, et cetera. She would do her room. In fact, I was not welcome in it, until the day she had another attack. I was the one to put the nitroglycerin pill in her mouth under her tongue. I called emergency, she was hospitalized, and then came home again. She then decided she

32

would start giving some antique dishes away to her daughters. Then she'd turn around and accuse me of stealing them. She totally forgot what she was giving away. For my part, I was pleased she was parting with these heirlooms. I'd washed and dusted them for 14 years or more. Furthermore, I thought it was nice for her to see her daughters enjoy the things.

Mike told me one evening that even though he resented Dickie, he missed him so we sat down and talked and cried. We visited Dickie most weekends. It took a long time to realize the stress that one handicapped child can put upon a family. Now we had time to do for the church, the community, et cetera. A terrific burden had been lifted.

I now had only my mother-in-law who continued to dog me with remarks like "Your children are not pink and white, blonde or blue-eyed. They're alright." Whenever I made an error in cooking or gardening, she made sure that part of Hanover knew all about it. However, as I got involved in church and community endeavors, people began to come to me and say, "How do you stand living with her?" I'd smile and carry on. My journey of faith didn't make me hate her. Instead I began to feel sorry for this unhappy woman.

I also thanked God constantly for endowing me with a great sense of humor because without faith and humor I don't think I could have made it. There were days, believe me, when I wanted to chuck it all, but I'm glad I didn't. I knew I'd be playing right into her hands. Bob, my husband, was worth sticking around for even if his mother didn't make the pop charts. Finally, after getting worse after another heart attack, she had to be put into a nursing home. She died with her last heart attack.

Bob and I watched as anything of any value such as jewelry and coins was removed from the house. I have no misgivings. We bought the house. Nothing in it, remember? Anyway, the last hurt was when every child in the family received a Bernat hand-hooked rug made by my mother-in-law except Bob because he married a foreigner. Years later when we visited Bob's brothers or sisters we'd see the familiar items that had been in our home. In my heart I'm glad we didn't keep any of it. Things are just things.

My Teaching Experiences

When Susie, the baby, was ten years old, my sister-in-law talked to me about considering taking a job team teaching at the Baptist Church. The church was opening a public kindergarten. The lead teacher was a lady from Cohasset. So I talked it over with Bob and decided to do it. It was mornings, and I'd be home before Susie arrived home. June and I clicked immediately. We had full attendance, and the school prospered. I really enjoyed working with the children and did that for some years until June decided it was time to move on.

My next venture was to apply as a teacher's aide at Salmond School in Hanover. I got the job and immediately was assigned primarily to Miss Rugman who taught 3rd grade. I also had other duties like playground and cafeteria duty. Once again, a deep friendship blossomed between Miss Rugman and me. I loved being with the children, helping with all subjects. After a while, the Reading Supervisor Mrs. Forman asked me to help her. She, too, was wonderful to me. She observed me and taught me a lot about the various tests. She told me I had a natural talent and should return to college and to study learning disabilities. So I went home and discussed that with my husband.

Learning to Drive!

First things first, I still didn't know how to drive. Bob was all for me going to college, but he said my first priority was to learn to drive. A girl friend took me Sundays to the Hanover High School parking lot for my first lessons. Bob would then take me out and criticize and yell at me the whole time. Ai-yah!! I would end up in tears. Bob offered me a job packing potato chips at his plant, so with that money I invested in Driving School. I never let on to him that I was taking driving lessons. It was my secret. Instead my dialogue would be, "If I ever get my license, will you buy me a car?" His answer would always be, laughingly, "Sure, I will, but you've got a long ways to go with just your Sunday lessons!" Ai-yah!!

Finally, my driving lessons were over. So that Sunday we went for our usual husband and wife lesson. Bob was still yelling at me about taking corners too wide, I was a disaster in the making at intersections, et cetera, et cetera. I never let on that in two days, I at 42 would be driving in Quincy for the Registry of Motor Vehicles! Needless to say, I was a nervous wreck. My turn. This was it. I passed with flying colors! I was excited. The only wrong thing I did was offer the registry inspector an apple—bribery! I didn't think that way. I couldn't wait to get home and call Bob at work to tell him the news. I did just that. Bob couldn't believe what he was hearing. The phone was silent for a while. True to his word, he bought me a new Chevy Nova, gold color. I was thrilled. I was driving. Was America ready for me?!

Going to College and Teaching

My next goal was to register for college. Learning disabilities (LD) was one of the prominent subjects in education at that time.

Boston University, Lesley, or Curry offered the best courses. I chose the easiest drive from home, Curry in Milton. Actually one of the greatest spokeswomen for learning disabilities Dr. Gertrude Webb and her assistant, Carol Wadell, were at Curry.

Bob was so supportive of me through all of this. It was hard caring for a family, working, going to college, studying, and writing papers, but I did it and graduated, and then went back into the school system in Hanover as an LD tutor. I loved every minute of it. The students I felt benefited from my tutelage, and my heart felt good. I know this deep sense of helping other people's children stemmed a great part from the incapability of not being able to help my own son learn. To this day, children I tutored and their parents, when we meet, have a special love and bond. We've never forgotten each other through the years. It's a great feeling that money can't buy. The children felt my love and they all improved and did well in school. They knew I was there just to help them and love them, and it did accomplish wonders.

In the mid-1980s I taught from 8:00 until 2:30, then still did retail from 3:00 until 9:00 pm. Finally Proposition 2 ½ cutbacks became a reality. After twelve and a half years I stopped tutoring, and did just retail in a woman's clothing store. Bob worked for the Water Department in Hanover, and I still did retail full time. All the children except for Dickie have been married, divorced, happily remarried, and have returned home to live at one time or another. One daughter Judi and son Tucker are still living with us. She never remarried.

Our Adult Children

Dickie is in a home situation with other retarded and handicapped adults. He's 42 years old and still can only scribble. His attention span is still zero, but he does the lowest level of

36

skill at a workshop for retarded. He is toilet trained, smokes, and speaks redundantly but fairly well. Mentally he is still a child. Most importantly though he has friends with the same capabilities.

Mike lives in New Jersey, very happily working in the trucking business. He has remarried and has a seven-year-old son by his prior marriage. His new wife has always been wonderful to his son, and that is a major plus. Coleen is a nurse, very beautiful and energetic.

Judi was a flight attendant for Eastern Airlines for twelve and a half years. She got married, miscarried, and when she got pregnant again the doctor advised her to stop flying if she wanted this pregnancy to come to term. Her maternity leave turned into never returning to flying as Eastern was in a major financial fiasco. She then worked in retail and was a bookkeeper for Sturbridge Yankee, a furniture and gift store, until it closed its doors. Now she is unemployed, but fulfilled as she's volunteering at the Wildlife Sanctuary in Hingham.

Susie remarried, and she went back to college. Her goal is to be an x-ray technician. Her new husband Jack is a love and is supportive of her. They are expecting their first child. The wonder of ultrasound reveals it's a "boy." She has Elaina, her eight and a half year old from her first marriage, who is thrilled with the idea of having a brother.

Us Retire? Never!

Bob and I were just saying we'll both be 65 years old and neither one of us thinks of retirement. We'll continue to work until we possibly can't. We feel extremely blessed, our grown family and grandchildren are a continued joy to us. They keep us young in mind and spirit.

I have a terrible sense of direction. Before I started college Bob took me for a trial run on how to get there, which exit, et cetera. It's a joke in our family even today because I just don't do expressways or freeways. I really am spoiled because work is five to ten minutes away. Trial runs done at night are great. I love that man for being so thoughtful. However, things do look different in the daylight. I got to class fine, but coming home I took a wrong exit.

Another day, there was a major accident on the expressway and the State Police waved everyone off. Well, I had no idea where I was going. I only knew one way to get to class. I never made class that day. I drove around the Blue Hills forever. Finally, I had to ask for help to get home. At one in the afternoon, telling people you're lost is a laughing experience to say the least. I got so I would remember three or four directions, and then I'd pull over for help again. In this way, I finally made it home. In this family, it's a given, don't go with Mum, you'd better drive her, because you'll never reach your destination if you rely on her.

I also have a poor sense of gadgets like microwaves or things, particularly in cars. It takes me forever to learn how to work half the stuff. Thank God for Bob. He takes the time to show me. I am a people person, and I feel I inherited the love of music and water color painting from Mum; intelligence, striving and determination from Dad.

Bob is a tenor, and I'm a soprano, and we both sing in the choir together. It's nice to do something together when our lives are so busy. Church has always been an intricate part of our lives. I feel secure that my cosmopolitan upbringing has broadened my view about religion and races. It is not an issue in this house.

I know living those long hungry years through a war prepared me for coping with a retarded son and a mother-in-law who never accepted me. Since her death, the family member who was mother's ally has become friendly to me. The rest of the family was always accepting of me; they all admitted to her vicious fault-finding nature. She was not a happy woman. She constantly blamed her husband for getting her pregnant ten times.

If duty bound sex can do that to a human being, I'm glad I'm not a part of that—love, spontaneity, enjoyment are my cup of tea. And I was brought up in a generation who never talked about sex. My mother never even told me about menstruation. I swam all morning, feeling terrible. My girlfriend had to explain it to me in the locker room.

It's a joke in our family. Here I was married, had children, and didn't really know that cats delivered their young like us. I was told they threw them up, and I believed it! Yi-yea!!

My Sister and Brothers

My sister Noemi and her husband Bill left for America first. Then when Bob and I arrived in Seattle, we thought it best to visit them in Oakland, California before we headed home to Boston.

My three brothers and parents were still in Hong Kong. After getting home to Hanover, my brothers wanted to come to the United States. They had all been in banking in Hong Kong. I had to sign some papers to ease their application into America, and it wasn't too long before they arrived here. My father decided to stay in Macau with his sister. Mum decided to come with the rest of the family.

Needless to say, they all settled down in California. The weather is more similar to Shanghai. Years later when I flew out for a nephew's wedding, I saw so many people from Shanghai. I'm convinced one half of Shanghai resides in California! I am the only member of the Machado family on the East Coast.

My sister had three sons Billy Jr., Bruce, and Brian and resided in Orinda, California. We would try and visit every few years with each other; likewise with my brothers or Bill and Noemi who would fly out with her boys to see us. However, Bill died in a tragic car accident and from that day on I have not seen my sister. I call her and send cards, but aside from any response from her, it is not there. A yearly Christmas card from her is it. I have never been invited out for a visit again.

My brothers get the same treatment, and they live in California beside her. She resides in Mirago, two of the brothers are in Los Angeles, and one in San Francisco. It's very sad, and we do not understand it. She wants nothing to do with her past. Unfortunately, she is robbing her three sons of additional love and friendship from us relatives by her selfishness. Nobody has hurt her in any way. It's her choice.

My brother Sonny (he's retired) and his family reside in San Francisco. Lulu is also in San Francisco. Mario is in Los Angeles. He has done very well for himself. He introduced soccer to the USA and did a lot of soccer broadcasting from Manchester, England. The first soccer magazine on the newsstand was co-owned by him. He does a lot of community work, bit parts in movies, hosts TV shows, and has won an Emmy for his TV show *Medic*.

My brothers and I keep in touch. In the first week of July we are all going to Vancouver for the "Old China Hands" reunion. Bob and I are getting very excited about it. To see people I grew up with, literally sat in class with and hung out with, is something I never envisioned happening to me. Life is wonderful, good and bad. I primarily enjoy every day, am thankful for my health, and for being alive.

Our Trip to Shanghai

In 1987, when Bob and I were married 40 years, our daughter Judi thought it would be a great gift for me especially to return to my birth place, Shanghai. She was still a flight attendant with Eastern so went ahead and made and paid for the whole trip. The local newspapers introduced us and took pictures of us. It was celebrity time again!!

Bob was thrilled with this gift of a return trip. I was, too, but I had mixed feelings. So much had happened, so much had changed. My feelings were affected after living through the war under the Japanese from 1937 to 1945. Nine years with no power, no water, not much food, and a lot of fear, and then the Americans liberated us. There were no foreigners, just Chinese. Under Communist rule most all of the city was renamed. It was a strange feeling. Tearing down many of the foreign architectural buildings there was no sense of freedom. Today in a poor Chinese home the working man or woman works ten hours a day, six days a week. In their home they are only allowed a 25 watt light bulb.

Even with my mixed feelings we went. It was a long flight. I must say that the people in Hawaii really do make you feel welcome. Flying into Hong Kong is beautiful, but the friendliness doesn't quite measure up to Hawaii. Then in Beijing (Peking to me) there was a very official attitude.

We loved Hong Kong. It reminded me a lot of Shanghai. Hong Kong was certainly more updated in architecture with new abundant building structures visibly in progress everywhere. One must remember that Hong Kong never closed its port or doors to the rest of the world just because Communism was in power. Shanghai did, and it's still trying to play that catch-up game.

In Shanghai I wanted to take Bob to see where I was born and lived and started kindergarten, but that kind of freedom never occurred. We did see two of the homes and apartments I lived in and also two of the schools I attended. I was happy about that.

We Arrive in Shanghai

My heart was beating, Shanghai had been home for me for 18 years. We landed at Hunjao Airport, newly rebuilt and renovated. It was the countryside where farmers lived when I was growing up. A few wealthy estates were scattered here and there. Now there are high rise apartments without the foreign influence in architecture. Most apartment buildings are square. Butcher shops still had a half side of a pig hanging from hooks and live chickens in cages. There were also eels, ducks, duck eggs, and fruit hawkers. 12.3 million people, and four million own bicycles. There were about 4,000 people per square mile. A bake shop was still very popular.

Everything that is important in the life of China is either painted, carved, or woven into fabric or carpet rugs. Labor is still cheap just like it was when I was a young girl. Young artisans work manually ten hour days for US $60.00 a month, six days a week painting, creating jewelry, and making rugs. The best quality wool rugs have 120 knots per square inch. Price is determined by the number of knots. Young ladies jump up and down to string the warp. Sculpturing the rugs is done with electric clippers and is considered one of the top positions.

Paper cutting and woodcarving are other important art forms. Paper cutting is a continuous free hand process in one cutting that makes two pictures simultaneously. It takes the artisan two minutes. Hand embroidered clothing is still an art form. The Art Centre was the home of the French Consulate in my day.

Nothing is ever wasted or thrown away until a use for it can be thought of. Tin cans that food was packed in are flattened, cut, painted into beautiful pictures, and then sold in the best stores.

The Chinese weight unit is called a "catty" and weighs a little more than one pound. Chinese New Year is the big holiday. The good luck color is red. Fuchsia thread or ribbon is woven into the braids of little girls, and red envelopes with gold characters are filled with money and are exchanged. Bowls of tangerines are on a table. One should pay off all old debts and solicitors will settle for a piece of jewelry instead of money to erase a debt.

Quail eggs, eels, squid, and snake are good for your gall bladder and rheumatism. Water had changed. Growing up everything had to be boiled or disinfected. The cosmopolitan ambience was gone from Shanghai. There was no more magic because all the foreigners had left. I can only recapture that feeling in my memory.

Shanghai Now and Then

Humanity is still happening on the streets without total freedom to speak or act as in the past. When I grew up people walked everywhere, and thousands lived on the streets. Now some of those thousands of pedestrians ride bicycles. I saw laundry still hung on bamboo poles and Chinese homes very dimly lit because they run their factories 24 hours a day and need the power for that.

The millionaire middle class—poor millionaires—bank their money in other countries and educate their children there also. Chinese currency was not dependable. From 1945 to 1946 there was a new government with new money. One American dollar was worth 60,000 Chinese yuan.

I grew up with a strong emphasis on family and respect, and I saw that a new dimension was added to the Chinese family because of birth control laws. The one child allowed per family is held with such love, with all things bestowed on this child even though the parents might come from modest means. That child would not be denied. One amazing factor in Shanghai is that they have a school for the gifted, and it is housed in the Cathedral School for Girls.

When I grew up you had to pay for your education; consequently only the middle class and wealthy were educated. Children who were around my age, eight years old to eleven years old, who were poor didn't go to school. If you were poor whatever talent your father had (example: carved furniture), the son would learn the trade from his father.

Many children helped earn some money by roaming the streets all day picking up cigarette butts and putting them into a container. At night at home they would crumble up all the tobacco, re-roll them into new cigarettes under their own brand name, and have them on sale the next morning on the sidewalk.

We had sidewalks in Shanghai but during the day they were covered by "hawkers" who sold their wares. Some of the beggars were genuine and others were impostors. They'd even pinch a baby to make him or her cry so you'd feel sorry and give them some money. For years I gave money to one particular beggar who had only one leg until late one night I saw him unfolding his other bandaged leg. A "hawker" definition: if you didn't have the money to rent a store you just spread a tablecloth with your wares. Come evening, one just tied up the wares, and if you didn't have a place to go, a straw mat was rolled out and you slept there.

The poor eat your garbage they're so hungry. If one needed a haircut, there was a walking barber shop complete with stool and you'd have a haircut or shave or ears cleaned right on the sidewalk while the rest of the world walked by. We also had a walking restaurant. He'd have noodles in a broth or pastry dumpling, and you'd sit and eat. Life literally happened on the street.

Another interesting factor was the pants Chinese babies wore. They had a huge slit that would appear whenever the child squatted and needed to use the toilet. And that, too, occurred anywhere. Toilet training was not a factor.

In the winter months these homeless people and beggars would move into entrance ways of homes or stores with the same bunch of rags and newspapers for their blankets. The colder it got, most people would wear a padded gown then top it with another gown lined with fur to windproof them. Most poor Chinese homes had no heat.

Because of the foreign influence women stopped having their feet bound. They also were going to beauty salons to have a permanent wave. Most females in China wore the one piece cheongsam, or black pants with a white or pretty blue top. The poor made their own shoes and slippers. Layers and layers of cloth were put together, and then a needle with thick twine thread was pushed back and forth until the sole was secure. Then the top piece and sole were hemmed by hand together. Voila the "flat." For the female some embroidery was always stitched onto the top piece.

Basically the neutral attitude was so accepting. If one was born poor, so be it. There was no bitterness. Your thing in life was to become a servant to a middle class or wealthy family. If a female, you were to be chosen as a concubine to a man who could afford as many as he so desired. His commitment was to house and care for Number Two wife as well as Number One.

No one asked questions or kept a record if a child or wife disappeared. It was no big deal. We had a police force and large jails, but they were used for other crimes. Corruption did abound. If your house was burning and you called the fire department, you were asked, "How much will you pay me for coming?" And if they did come, they helped themselves to the items not burned. You came away with the feeling of what did I gain by calling the fire department? Most people solved their own problems or crimes without the police or fire department. We had traffic lights. The only difference was no one paid any attention to them in those days.

If you were giving a piano to someone miles away, two men would appear to move it, and not with a truck! They'd sing the same song "Eh-how-eh-how," stop for lunch on the road, and get there eventually. They truly believed singing "Eh-how-eh-how," lightened the load. More oriental psychology!

Children are special. Couples are allowed only two children. A couple with one child is ensured income and housing. A second child eliminates that privilege. A third child puts that child at the bottom of the list for school, plus a penalty of ten percent of one's income until the child is fourteen years old.

Growing up, the poor always seemed to have large families. On the sidewalk every day you would see straw baskets. If you heard a sound, it would be a little girl. The poor had put the baby out to freeze, simply because it was one more mouth to feed. Many became blind from the cold. A male child was held in higher esteem. They felt a boy would grow up, work, and help support the family to survive, whereas, a girl would either get married or become a concubine.

Enter the missionaries!!! God bless them. They came to China to teach God's love, and they began to pick up these babies who were thrown away. With the results two large orphanages sprang up. They not only showed God's love, they lived it, and Christianity took hold. Prior to the missionaries, Buddhism was reverent. Worshippers went to the temple, leaving fruit, incense, and paper money to their Gods of Fertility, Happiness, Evil, et cetera. Shanghai's famous Lungwah Pagoda is over 4,000 years old. During the war one of the concentration camps was near there.

The "Race Course" was the only large piece of green in the heart of the city. Before the war, horse racing was an important pastime for the middle class and the wealthy. During one of the American airplane raids a bomb fell on the famous Nanking Road near the Wing-On Company and the Sincere Company. My mother was trapped there. Luckily she had no bodily harm. My oldest brother Lulu had to work on the disaster, loading the dead on trucks. He couldn't eat for a long time. Nausea dogged him.

47

There is a power plant across the Whangpoo run by soft coal, which creates a lot of cinders. I also went to another concentration camp in Pootug. The mouth of the river is 30 miles across. The channel is shallow so cargo is barged upstream to Shanghai. In the old days opium smuggling took place here.

During the war the pedicab came into being. Instead of the man running in front as in a rickshaw, he peddled a bicycle. There were single ones and double ones and should it rain the pedicab was complete with a little see-through square so you could see where you were going. You had to bargain on a price to your destination before you got in. Likewise with the rickshaw, you had to state your destination, and then bargain on the price.

It was not a good idea to wear too much valuable jewelry if you didn't know the ins and outs of Shanghai. If the coolie knew you were a new foreigner chances are you'd be taken to an alleyway and be robbed. I've known of cases where if the ring didn't slip off easily, the finger would be chopped off. Earrings were pulled right through a pierced hole. People were so hungry that stealing was a daily occurrence. Needless to say pawn shops did a thriving business.

The farmers coming into Shanghai dressed differently. They wore wrap around cotton skirts over their trousers. The wheel barrow they pushed was wooden with one large wheel in the center and on one side they'd tie the produce for the market, and for balance the farmer would tie his wife/child and put more produce on the other. After the produce was sold, the man deserved part of the ride home, and his wife would accommodate him. They lived very simply outside the city. Their home had few windows, no doors to speak of, and a mud floor. Chickens, pigs, and ducks ran in and out, all in perfect harmony. It was a hard life. The farmers fertilized their fields with human manure.

Most Chinese houses had no sanitation system. Instead they had large wooden pots. These pots were put on the sidewalk for the man with the "honey cart" to pick up, another hard, thankless job.

My Thoughts in 2009

I am 81 years old! I love America! I love being alive and thankful for each day. So much has changed. The most traumatic and sad thing was the loss of my Bob in 2006. It was so quick. He called me right after I checked on him to exit the room. He was having difficulty breathing. I pressed 911, and told him to hang on as I had to call Judi. His last words to me were, "Don't leave me!" When I returned after calling Judi, he had slumped backwards to the wall. Judi arrived with Jay. She started CPR and I moved his leg. It felt so heavy!! I knew it wasn't good. Firemen arrived and they worked on him awhile. They put him on a gurney and took him to South Shore Hospital. We followed. I remember feeling so cold and numb. Granted his health had been declining—pace maker, asthma, legs, so many things. He had to take over 20 to 30 pills of some sort. He needed a cane to walk.

Bob always came to Merchant's Row to have lunch with me every day. I worked at Potpourri Designs. This lunch date happened after he had cancer in the one kidney which was removed, plus his retirement. Per usual, everyone in the Mall got to know him and loved him. They even had a book for all to sign and write in when he passed.

Bob was an amazing man. He took such good care of me. He was a great father and loved his family and grandchildren. I loved his high standards, his thoughtfulness, and his kindness. What an amazing chef and baker. He loved his vegetable garden. It was

49

magnificent. He grew everything simply to give it away to everyone he liked and visited with. He loved his truck, and played classical tapes. He sang in the choir until his legs gave out. I still sing in the choir at UCC. This choir is outstanding. The director Karen Harvey was one of Bob's special people. I love music, it really helps one's soul and makes you feel so good.

I do miss him so much, but I do talk to him constantly about the news of the day. I mow all the lawn since before I used to just help him. He had a ride on and I had the walk on. I love having it look good. I'm sure he's proud of me. I'm also not working so much. The economy is really bad, so I read, paint, and try to keep busy. I find I used to get upset about my hours being cut, but since Bob's gone I just deal with it. As long as I can pay my bills, that's fine. It has taken forever clearing up the paper work. Thank God for Susan (from church) to help me. There's a lot I have to do now since Bob's gone: banking, groceries, et cetera, but with God's help I'm doing it.

Susie and Judi are wonderful to me. They are still grieving. I feel I'm dealing with my grief by living in this home with so much of Bob and my memories around me every day. I feel the love. Granted I have humor. It's good to laugh about yourself. Why not? I tap dance around the kitchen island by myself too! I have good friends, neighbors. Helen Kelley always takes me to lunch. The O'Rourke's and Shirley Mesheau are the best neighbors.

I start my day with twenty to thirty minutes of exercise. I put my coffee on, and then I pray and meditate. I always thank God at night for another great day and for His love and care for me. Looking back on my life I know God has touched me many times. I am pretty happy most of the time, optimistic, love people, my grandkids, and children. Small things can set me off on a happy high.

Dickie is 62 and struggling with health issues. I've prayed about this and only God knows best. Children's Hospital never thought he would live beyond 40 years. We do have a spot for him with Bob and me at the cemetery. This winter has been the hardest for me without Bob. Probably the amount of snow and the economy that kept me housebound has contributed to the mood. I've painted 26 pictures to boot, and I must say at 81 I'm a better artist!!

My brother Mario is not good. He has Parkinson's. However I'm sure his mental attitude has a lot to do with it. You have to be up and fight it, not give in. I told him so many things, to listen to music, to dance. It affects a different part of your brain. God, I dance every day. Alas, he won't even try. Sonny is good. He's very close to his family and never complains. Marie his wife is into going on "pilgrimages" (Israel) et cetera instead of Hong Kong shopping. My sister Noemi is in an apartment in Orinda on the 6th floor and doing well. She'll be 87 years old. She keeps busy and is still driving.

I really love my home. It's so comforting, so handy to everything. It's been in the Sides family forever. One of the sad memories was when Bob's father died shortly after I arrived in America. His mother insisted on having a Masonic service at home. So Bob and I and Dickie had to leave and sleep at Spider and Marion's. It was horrendous for me to see a casket in the dining room, then to have to serve a ton of fish chowder to everyone after the service. Bob was none too pleased. He said he would never join the Masons!! Actually it was my first funeral, and it was all so new to me. After all it was America. The casket, spooky red lights, flowers, open with his father was scary to me. I'd never do that!

I have to say I'm so proud of my grandchildren. I love them. Each one adds a dimension to my life—Tucker, Elaina, Ryan, Lia, Sean and Brandon. I try to help when I can with support and hugs and tell them I love them. Bob would cry at anything special they accomplished.

One conversation I had with my youngest brother Mario was that our mother never hugged us or showed affection. I agreed with him. She never did. She felt she wanted to do her thing. She had the children, and that was enough. Baby-Amah could take care of us. Then when there was no Baby-Amah, and I had to do everything. She was never home. Many people called her "Marie, the Gad About."

My sister was excellent at everything she endeavored. I was strong in English, fair in math. In fact my teacher in English really liked me and my essays. I was the reader to the class. She and one other teacher paid for me to join the Brownies then Girl Scouts. I was in the Swallow patrol. I enjoyed all that and had a lot of friends who invited me to their homes. We had to wear uniforms to school, so everyone knew what school you went to. It's the British way.

After graduation, I went to Business School with my friends. Then we all got jobs, saw each other whenever, either at the YMCA or visiting on weekends or movies. My sister belonged to a more private club, "The Lusitano." Her peers and friends were wealthier and older. In fact, many of them didn't even know Noemi had a "kid sister."

I was best friends with an Italian girl Anita Permé and two sisters who were Doris and Vera Pribram. We all lived in the same apartment complex on Bubbling Well Road. Doris and Vera escaped from "Hitler." They were German Jews. Their mom and dad were both doctors. They had a dog so we went walking all the time. Our life was always walking to everything, miles and miles to school, church, the Y, to each other's homes. Many of my friends lived in "French Town," lots of walking from my house in the "International Settlement." I still like to walk!

Bob and I loved going to the China Hands reunion. I never thought I'd see those friends again after the war, but I did, and I loved it. Judi and Tucker came with us to Vegas and San Francisco. Vancouver "China Hands" is no more, everyone is older and it took a tremendous amount of work to get 1,200 to 1,500 people together. Beautiful while it lasted, so many said to me, "Hey, you turned out okay." My sister was the popular known one. I was known as "Miss Wall Flower." My mother called me "Cinderella." When we had dances at the Y to get acquainted there was a "Paul Jones." Boys formed one circle, and girls the other. When the music stopped you had to dance with the boy in front of you. Every boy sighed sadly when he got me, so I mostly ended up as a wallflower watching. So I definitely was a late bloomer. It wasn't until I started to work when I was 16 or 17 years old that boys did notice me.

I remember the Japanese Flagship "Izuma" coming into the harbor. There was shooting, scaring everyone for miles, and causing devastation. "The Bund" was a beautiful waterfront area with huge banks, British Embassy, Palace Hotel, Cathay Hotel, shipping companies, and a park. Further down over the Garden Bridge were the Broadway mansions, Russian Embassy, Capitol Theatre, and the New Asia Hotel. No one went out after four in the afternoon during the war. It wasn't safe. All the stores boarded up, so there was no shopping. You were lucky to stay in and survive.

The Japanese always surprised everyone with house or apartment inspections. They would pound your door with fixed bayonets. Once in they would search all your mattresses, closets, wardrobes, and drawers to make sure you didn't have a radio that we were not allowed. If caught you were dragged off to the "Bridge House," a huge apartment complex they made into a torture house. My brother Lulu's best friend Jimmy Ladd who drove a huge Harley Davidson was taken one night simply because he was a BBC newscaster. They hung him upside down and burned him forever so that he would say he was a spy. My brother got word finally at the end as Jimmy landed in the hospital and died.

In Shanghai early in the morning the vendors put their wares out on the sidewalk to see. This peanut vendor was there every day as we headed to school. One morning he spat and it landed on a Japanese officer's boot. The officer took out his samurai sword, pushed the peanut vendor to the ground and chopped off his head. I was petrified. Blood was everywhere. They were cruel.

Another thing they did was have barbed wire fences. Whenever the American planes appeared, the Japanese shot across the street every 200 to 300 yards so that we pedestrians would be stuck in whilst anti-aircraft boomed and shrapnel hit the people. American planes flew high altitudes so anti-aircraft couldn't touch them.

Next, they decided to dig fox holes in the sidewalk every 200 yards for a last stand within the city. Because they were big holes, people fell into and broke their legs. Babies were thrown in to die.

We had our own tailor in good times. You'd go to the fabric store and buy the yards necessary. The tailor came to your home, and you showed him a picture of what you wanted and he made it. He came again to pin you at a fitting, and then it was done. We also had a manicurist who came Sunday mornings to do my dad's nails and those of anyone else in the family. My dad always looked so dapper going to the embassy. He wore grey spats, a grey Homburg hat, a suit, and an overcoat when chilly, and he had a walking cane.

We went to Sacred Heart Church before the war. Then we went to Christ the King on Rue Bourgeat, French Town. Bob and I were married at Christ the King, and so were my sister and Bill Leonard. I went to Thomas Hanbury School for Girls. My brothers went to St. Xavier's. My best friends Vera and Doris went to L'Ecole Françoise, and Anita went to Public School for girls. A lot of boys went to Jeanne D'Arc. There was no co-education. There was also Cathedral School for Girls. The American school was the only school with co-education and no uniforms. Life was good in pre-war days, but things change on a dime. One has to cope, adjust every day. We had to learn the Japanese language in school while they were in power.

I remember being so hungry some days. I knelt and prayed for long periods. We were allowed a half pound of bread from the Russian bake shop with a coupon. Someone decided to put stones and worms in the flour so you had to take all that out before eating. We all lived day to day, hoping for the end of the war. We only had three beds for six people, so three slept on the floor. I was the one to do the scrubbing and sweeping of the floor. We didn't even have an ice box (refrigerator). I learned that major changes in my life happened, and how to bear and live through it. Material things disappear. I was sad to lose my home and life I had, but I had to move on. I prayed a lot.

My two brothers kept me busy. Mario was so cute. Everyone wanted to adopt him. Sonny was quiet and serious. He even thought he wanted to be a priest, and he did until he had to go to solitary. He quit. At some point after the Americans freed Shanghai, they left. A Lt. Bailey wanted to adopt Mario, and my mother agreed. I'm sure she was given some money. I didn't understand it, and my sister to this day holds that against Mum. The outcome of the adoption was Mario lived in California, and went to St. John's Military Academy for a few years. He then wanted to come back to Shanghai. The uncle who gave me a sweet potato also left my mother a considerable amount of money when he died.

After the Japanese left, the Americans came. Life was good for a while. Then the Communists began to infiltrate and things became a hassle again. Anti-American, anti-foreign feelings seeped in. My sister and I left for America leaving the family in Shanghai. They finally escaped the Communists to Hong Kong. They lived there until they came to America, all except my dad in Macau. He taught college in Hong Kong. He took his evening walk every day and was hit by a motorcyclist at dusk and died. I'm sad that I never saw my dad again.

I did see the rest of the family. Mum was the cook and lived at the rectory in San Francisco. She was my Mum, but I never felt loved, only fear from all the beatings I received. I'm sure most of my brothers didn't feel loved or my sister. Mum was not into that scenario. I know it shaped me into being a loving, caring mom. I feel loved by Bob and my girls and my grandchildren and friends. There is nothing like love!!

Every day I thank God for my life. It's so good to be alive. And when the sun shines, it makes my heart so happy. I remember coming home from the market one day without the meat or ribs

Mum told me to buy. I did buy them, but the thieves stole them from my basket. So when she questioned me, she was angry. She thought I took the money and bought some snack. So she took a heavy glass bottle (we used these bottles after boiling the water so it was drinkable) and hit me. The bottle broke and cut a main vein in my elbow. Bleeding and crying, I ran to the Fango Institute close by. The doctor prepared mud packs and helped me with my cut and bandaged me up. Mum did nothing. This reflection is how I know God wanted me to live and carry on.

I was always hungry. My friends Vera and Doris Kemp had some corned beef in a can left over and offered it to me. I ate it and got food poisoning. The doctor had one last vial of penicillin, and he injected me. It saved my life. I was sick a long time, and went down to 87 pounds. Isn't it amazing that I got the last vial of penicillin? With the harbor blocked nothing came in. You used what you had, period. I was blessed once again.

Towards the middle of the war my parents separated. So my brothers and I visited my father every weekend. He lived just down the street from us. My sister to this day feels Mum was such a hindrance to my father's career. She never attended anything pertaining to the embassy, lectures, publishing of a book, et cetera with my dad. She always was gone doing her thing. Parts of Shanghai saw her more than her family. She never bothered with us. We had to fend for ourselves. She had rules galore!! Even at 16 I had to ask permission to go to a party at a friend's house. Midnight was curfew until you're 21. She would be waiting at the door at midnight. It wasn't worth getting another beating and being punished to stay out after midnight.

I remember Mario, Sonny, and I were home alone, and we were hungry so we jimmied Mum's cabinet where she locked up money and valuables. I took two rolls of pennies and went and bought snacks for the three of us. We paid for it dearly. Sonny's hand was put on a fire and burned. I was beaten. Mario was spared. We never did that again. No wonder we were scared stiff of Mum. She was bad.

Bob was so thoughtful. He had this fabulous vegetable garden that he planted and tended in the backyard. The girls thought he should have a veggie stand out front. "No," he said, "I like to leave a bag of veggies and visit with each person." That's what gave him the most joy from it all! He also would turn my car around and back it into the garage for me, knowing that I was the worst backer-upper out of the garage in the whole world. After he moved my car, I'd just have to drive forward to go to work.

Tucker graduated summa cum laude from Suffolk on August 25, 2010. He interned at Price Waterhouse. I love him. Four years without Bob. Guess you just try to live on the best you can. I guess that hole in my heart is always going to be there, and he would want me to carry on.

I have handed in my keys to Potpourri Designs. I don't want to be on call any more. The truth is, they have no intention to use me, but don't want to fire me, so I needed to hand in my keys. It finalizes it for me mentally. Now I know there will be no more finances coming from there! I somehow still have to pay taxes and bills, but I love being in this house so I will figure something out. The girls are wonderful to me. My friend Helen takes me for lunch. We love soup at Panera. Shirley is a great neighbor and Bobby and Sue O'Rourke are, too. We're having a yard sale on Sunday, August 20, 2010. I'll try to sell some paintings and stuff. Hope it goes well. Susie's helping; also Judi, Lia, Elaina, Bobby.

September 2010 Dickie will be 63!! It's amazing that Susie's Ryan will graduate in June from St. John's Prep. Elaina is a wonderful artist. Finally Lia starts 7th grade and already looks forward to going to college. Tucker starts at Suffolk on his Master's. He needs to live at the house one more year. I continue to do well with God's blessings. Choir starts upon the 23rd. That'll be super. The yard sale was a success, and I sold six paintings.

I went to church on Sunday and sang in the "pick up choir." It felt so-o-o good. This summer I've missed church quite a bit, but I felt it's important to go to Ogunquit or Susie's to spend time with family. It really renews my spirit. God knows that.

Summer 2016

In this year 2016, I am so excited to be involved in writing about my life. Upon reflection, prayer was always a part of me. However, my prayers all started to be written because our choir always had a special time for prayer during each rehearsal. I am so thankful that this choir felt my prayers deeply enough to speak to me about them.

Thanks to Pam and Carolyn and this choir with Karen Harvey as our director who have touched my heart. They are God's angels on this earth, each one of them. Because of them my life has been blessed. To be allowed to sing with them has been an honor. Truthfully I don't read music. I don't know a *do* from a *la*. I follow totally by ear and memory. I fake what I don't know!! I'm sure I'm not fooling Karen, but she's been so kind to let me sing. So till I get deaf, I plan to continue singing as I love music. My soul needs it, and I love the members of this choir.

Norma at Kiangwan Airfield
1945

Bob and Norma at Kiangwan Airfield
1945

Bob at the Race Course
1945

Wedding Day November 29, 1947

Norma and Bob's Wedding Day
Dad   Doris   Bob   Norma   Noemi (sister)   Sonny (brother)

Bob, Dickie and Norma
Minot Beach, Scituate, Massachusetts
1949

Dickie, Mike, Judi and Susie
Desk carved in Shanghai, China in 1947
Hanover, Massachusetts
1959

**Norma Sides
January 1996**

**Bob and Norma Sides
January 1996**

WHEN YOU NEED A PRAYER

Take a moment. Relax.
Think about the prayer you need.
You know about Norma's life
and you will come to know her in prayer.

Worship Leader Prayers
Faith
Music
Trust and Comfort
Being Thankful
Family and Friends
Guidance
Outlook on Life

Each new prayer begins with one of the above headings and if
more than one page long ends with the image below.

And now, as Norma always says before she begins,

"Will you bow your heads in prayer with me?"

WORSHIP LEADER PRAYERS

August 11, 1985

"For everything there is a season
and a time for every matter under heaven.
I was glad when they said unto me,
let us go into the house of the Lord."

Ecclesiastes 3:1

This morning, like so many other mornings, I want to thank God for being here and for having the opportunity to feel the Holy Spirit transmitted from Dave to us. I am blessed to be among people who show a real expression of faith, a deep and meaningful commitment, and who constantly move as witnesses to their love for God. This church is not only person-centered, but task-centered as well, involved in job, community, and the world.

God loves each one of us, faults and all. Isn't it great to be alive and loved? Like so many here, we have all felt joy or heartache, or have had to face a crisis. In China, the word crisis is made up of two characters:

"way" meaning danger
"gee" meaning opportunity

So in the Chinese language, the character of crisis depends on what we see in the experience or disaster. Or could it be an opportunity for building one's character?

As I look back on upon my life, I know I could not have made it without You, Lord. Very early in my life You touched me.

Through 8 ½ years of war and hunger, You sustained me through hours of prayer. That prepared me for my first born, who was born handicapped and also prepared me for a mother-in-law who never accepted me simply because I was a foreigner.

I thank You, Lord, for not making me bitter, but instead You blessed me with a good husband and family. You channeled my heartaches into positive action by reaching out and by teaching and loving other handicapped children. I felt joy again.

The journey through life is meaningful because of You, God.

Love requires an open mind and a free heart.

Each of us has our own uniqueness to express it.

So when the question is asked.

How have I believed?

And how have I loved?

Lord, let me have the right answer.

Amen.

WORSHIP LEADER PRAYERS

July 12, 1987

Will you bow your heads in prayer with me? Jesus said, "Blessed are your eyes for they see, and your ears for they hear."

Dear God in this hour of worship hear us as we pray. Bless each one here and those who are not. Help me in my day to day living to grow like that mustard seed, using the recipe of love.

Love has nine ingredients: patience, kindness, generosity, humility, courtesy, unselfishness, good temper, sincerity, and guilelessness. It's a tough recipe to follow, Lord! My father always said to me, "Look into a person's eyes, and it will tell you the "heart" of the person." He was right!

Bless me with that perception when it unfolds itself like a brand new day. Even though it might be just a hug to a customer I deal with or Bob planting a little flower garden for our granddaughter. It started with love and was nurtured to bloom in love. This body of believers in His church is like that! They really look with love in their eyes and hear the many concerns here and around the world. That's Your way, Lord, and I really would like to grow from that mustard seed branching out into a healthy tree.

You touched me, Lord, very early in life. I will never forget the day of the first bombing attack on Shanghai. The streets were full of panic stricken people, running to get over the bridges to safety on the other side. My neighbors shouted that I should throw a few things into a sheet, gather up my two baby brothers, and escape with them. Mum was helping my two aunts move to the French sector. One servant had left, and Baby-Amah was at the market. I was alone and had to make a decision. So I knelt and prayed. That time the answer came immediately. I took my two baby brothers and hid under the bed until Baby-Amah and my big brother made their way home to us.

Thank You, Lord for the beauty of each day and for being here. Thank You for being my faithful and forgiving Friend. Thank You, Lord for the dimension of sorrow and joy in my life. But most of all, thank You, Lord for making me need a quiet, peaceful time with You. Amen.

WORSHIP LEADER PRAYERS

June 18, 1989
Father's Day

Dear God,

Today we come to You with many concerns. One that is uppermost in our hearts and minds is the recent massacre in Tiananmen Square. Why is it that innocent, unarmed people always get killed? I feel sad that people have to live in fear of their lives once again due to a power or a government.

Years ago my father, a diplomat, said to me, "Norma, please don't discuss politics in your letters to me as they are being censored. I have to live in China until I can get out." Can you believe this very same dialogue is going on today for the students and people who have to live there against a government's policy?

I lived with curfew, no electricity, and a tub of water for six to last all day for everything. My family was one of the lucky ones. We had to go to the store to buy our hot water. Don't they know it doesn't work? I have lived through it. It doesn't work. Tanks can't kill dreams. AK-47s can't kill hope. Martial law can't kill desire and unity, and propaganda can't kill the truth.

If we, as Your people, truly believe in the example You have set for us, we know that only You, and Your forgiving constant love can sustain everything.

I know with You in my heart, I can live each day.
With You in my heart, fear can turn into strength.
With You in my heart, hope gets renewed.

71

Let the students in China feel our love and concern. Let them know that there will be a better tomorrow because there is!

I am standing here thanks to You, God. I live in a country that is absolutely fantastic where people are so loving, thoughtful, and caring. In this place there's no fear of the government or policy killing you or torturing you because you might not agree. Words can't express my joy with this place. Home is where the heart is, and I thank You, God for making me a person with a heart. Because when my heart is with You, my whole being sings and my mind feels good!! The heart and the mind go together. Thank You, God. Amen.

WORSHIP LEADER PRAYERS

February 23, 1997

Dear God,

Here I am again talking to the special person in my life. I could never have made it this far without You. It's as simple a truth as that. As I reflect upon my life, I see Your spirit and hand at work, touching me, pulling me, from doubt and sadness to renewed faith.

Sue talked about "mountain top" moments. You have taken me there many times. From the time I was nine years old at the start of the war in China, living scared and hungry for years, You sustained me. When I was food poisoned and dropped down to 87 pounds and received the last vial of penicillin in the whole city from a German doctor, it was You again. Through heart-broken days, many spent at Children's Hospital with a severely retarded and handicapped child along with a mother-in-law who disliked me because I was a foreigner and was not white with blue eyes, You were there beside me.

When St. Coletta's told me they couldn't keep my son anymore for reasons beyond my control, I didn't have anyone to turn to except You. I was new to America. I prayed every day in June and July and by early August doubts started entering my mind, me of little faith! Later in August as I was housecleaning one day, bang, out of nowhere, Your answer came. You said, "Call your selectman at the Town Hall and tell him your predicament with your child who has nowhere to go." I looked up the number and called the selectman's office and told him my story. He listened and then answered, "I will go right into the State House for you!" When Bob came home, I told him what I'd done. He thought I'd lost my mind!

No way! God, You opened doors for me. Both the selectman and my State Representative worked hard to get my son into the Paul Dever State School. Financially they geared the cost to our level, too. "Mountain top moments," "Ai-yeah," as they say in China! That selectman and I still have a special bond.

Three years ago Bob had cancer of the kidney. Once again, You blessed us. The kidney and the cancer were removed, and the cancer had not spread. But because of it, Bob touches base with me for lunch every day. Isn't that wonderful?

Your spirit continues. Ed spoke extensively about Mr. Aaron Feuerstein, president of Malden Mills. I was so impressed by what he did for his employees. In 1995 Malden Mills was destroyed by fire. Aaron Feuerstein told his employees they would stay on the payroll during the rebuilding process. I wrote to him, and he answered. He thanked me for my kind letter and said, "People who possess the same heart as Micah, when he said, 'He has told you, O Man, what is good, and what God really wants from you: Only that you act justly, with loving-kindness and walk humbly with thy God.' " I admire and respect that man. He is all those things, a living legend of goodness.

Bob and I will be married 50 years this November. We have four great kids and five grandchildren whom we adore and love, and for this I thank You, God.

This is the start of Lent and to me, it's a time of reflections. It's a time to look inward into my heart to see where I am and where I have fallen short or sinned and strive to do it better. My heart and mind must be in harmony. Thank You for making me a caring

74

person, for giving me a sense of humor, for showing loving kindness to people every day at work or at home, and to be grateful and happy for every day, and also to just be alive. You have woven an unbreakable thread throughout my life. It's a one-of-a-kind piece of art. It's no wonder I spend each day before bedtime saying, "Thanks, God, You are so great!"

WORSHIP LEADER PRAYERS

April 29, 2001

Will you join me in prayer.

Dear God, You are the one I turn to in prayer first thing at the start of each day. This quiet time with You is so special. It sets my mind and fills my heart with joy. It hones my awareness and gratefulness to be alive! You are the one who helps me smile, to be cheerful, happy to go to work, and to interact with other people. I feel at peace.

Three years ago You touched my life again. One of my coworkers brought in an article about breast self-examination and left it on the back counter. Each time I used either computer or the MC/Visa machine, I passed by the article. Being 70 at the time, I had never even thought that was necessary. That night I did a self-examination and found a tumor. It was cancer and had to be removed. Thanks to the people of this church who came to my home to visit and pray with me. I can't say enough for the Visiting Nurses' Association who came daily and reassured me I was healing. I am doing well because of the spiritual power that was added to the medical expertise.

You know, God, with my zest for life and enthusiasm that is part of me, I felt compelled to adopt three to five cancer patients and nurture them with love, cards, and calls. I needed to give back that which I was given. Deep friendships have developed with the patients and families because of this. It really works, and it is so important. Do you believe Hallmark sends me checks? Isn't that wonderful? After my first check up, I sent my surgeon flowers to thank him for all he did for me. You know me, God,

76

better than anybody else, and because of You, my heart is filled with love.

Some of you who know me know that I was born in Shanghai, China and survived World War II under the Japanese. From nine years of age through my teens, I was a very quiet girl. My sister was the total opposite of me. She was beautiful, a debutante who enjoyed society. I stayed home, did the housework, and took care of my two young brothers. I was called "Cinderella."

In 1945, the Americans freed us. I applied for a job at the Kiangwan Airfield. There this Cinderella met her prince. However, I had to fight for my prince, as his mother was not in favor of our marriage. Bob and I decided it would be best if he returned to the United States, and I'd get there sometime. Our parting was very sad. After a few days, I knew I had made a huge mistake by giving in to his mother's wishes.

Time was against me. He was on his way to Japan, half way home. So I called my girlfriend who was secretary to the commanding general at the airbase to set up an appointment with him. We met, he listened, and then said, "I'll do all I can to help you." The commanding general took action. Every pilot, ham operator, and teletype message carried, "Find Sgt. Sides." They all checked back with me every day. All the airmen wanted to know, "Who was Norma, this civilian that the Air Force was working so hard for?" Finally he was located and phoned me. That was a happy day!

Life demands a decision, sometimes not immediately. This church is undergoing an unsettled, anxious decision time, and whatever the decision, I am confident the people of this church will choose the right road. Why? Because we have three blessings to start off with.

1. Chapin. He truly radiates the Spirit of God. Can't you almost feel the Holy Spirit at work here? By having him at the helm of our ship, we won't pull up nets without fish.
2. Karen. What a God-given talent she has. She is the one who fills our souls with music and lends meaning to the words.
3. You. Do you know how exceptionally wonderful you are? Caring, giving, and doing all in the name of God's love. You make this place vibrant and alive.

Bob and I have been coming here for 23 years. Worshipping here has been very meaningful to us. Without it, life would have a huge void. Nothing can take its place. Every one of us is loved by God. Accepting His love, gives my life purpose, gives me strength through heartaches and pain, and renews my home when my soul and spirit are weak.

I love this thought of God that I conjure up every day:

Listen. Come. Hide your face in My embrace.
My strong arms will carry you.
Rest in My love, keep close to Me.
Your burdens I will take on Me, and
bear you up on eagle's wings.
And He will raise you up on eagle's wings. Bear you
on the breath of dawn. Make you to shine like the sun.
And hold you in the palm of his hand.

WORSHIP LEADER PRAYERS

TRIBUTE TO BOB

November 4, 2006

My Tribute to Bob

I want to thank each one of you who came today. You are Bob's family and an extended one. He cared and loved you all. He always shared his thoughts with me about you. He truly was a great husband, father, and friend. He touched so many lives. He stood for honesty and for doing anything to the best of your ability or don't do it! His values never faltered. He was an example in this world, touched by God. He loved his church, his home, and his family. He took pride in his care of me, his garden, his family, his home, and his friends. No one can ever replace his spot on this earth. He was a good man.

Quietly you came into my life …
Openly you shared yourself with me …
Gently you drew me close, always closer …
Tenderly you touched a place deep within my heart …
Gratefully I celebrate the beauty of each moment and day that I
shared with you …

I miss you deeply and love you forever. I miss your hugs, but I feel one every time I mow the lawn. One of the best things I have done in my life was to marry you, and I try to focus on those 58 years.

I want to share this poem with you.

"There Is a Strength"

There is a strength that makes you able to master headaches and trials or the greatest disaster. You don't always win. You might bow to defeat, but there is a strength.
It puts you back on your feet, though your body grows frail, and you must suffer pain.
There is a strength that is always the same.
It doesn't depend on how much you can cope, for you hold a treasure that renews all your hope. Ever there when you need it, and seeing you through.
Your strength comes from God, who lives within you.

If anyone would like to say anything in honor of Bob, please do so now. We will close by joining hands and saying the Lord's Prayer.

WORSHIP LEADER PRAYERS

May 13, 2007
Mother's Day

This morning I want to thank God for each one of you being here. Happy Mother's Day to all of you. I am blessed to be among people who have a deep faith and commitment as a witness of their love for God and who are so involved in family, community, and the world. So like a mother with her family that love of God within our hearts motivates us with love for our children and friends.

Love requires an open mind and a free heart. Isn't it wonderful to know that God loves each one of us? We are all welcome in this journey of life. The Holy Spirit is alive! It's not an easy task to be a mother. You are the one who teaches the values day to day. You are the nurturer, cook, laundryman, driver, et cetera. Most times it's so rewarding to see the result within the family. For me, I love telling my children and grandchildren, "I love you," or giving them a hug. I'm sure it's because my mother never said or did that to any of the five of us. That's so sad.

It's also sad that today is the anniversary of Bob's death. One year, where did it go? I wouldn't be standing here if I didn't have the support of you all, Chapin, the choir and my family. Bob was an amazing man. He loved this church and all of you. He was a great father and friend and husband. He took pride in his care of me, his garden, and his family. He stood for honesty and for doing anything to the best of your ability, or don't do it!

He was touched by God. Since his death, memory has become my partner. I make it, hold it, and I dance with it. I talk to God and Bob constantly. It's my guaranteed asset of my human life.

It's my set of "hard-earned tools" to use and propel me forward with my accumulated skills for life. I knew kindness, thoughtfulness, and humor are important facts to life's story. Always with God it makes life good in spite of a huge loss.

Quietly you came into my life …
Openly you shared yourself with me …
Gently you drew me close, always closer …
Tenderly you touched a place deep within my heart …
Gratefully I celebrate the beauty of each moment and day that I
shared with you.

FAITH

Dear God,

We can't always have sunshine along life's path, but we can always count on Your love no matter what. Remind us each day to give thanks to You for being alive another day.

Never leave kind words unspoken. Smile, that makes your heart sing. It prepares you for whatever comes each day. Be a giver and sharer. Take moments belonging just to you. It refreshes your being. That's important.

God is always listening. He truly holds your heart in His hands. Sometimes we get so busy we forget to say "I love you." Remember to tell someone how special they are, or give a hug, or ask if there is something you can do to help. I have learned that the simple little things in life are the truest wealths of life and friendship.

We each have our own journey, lived one day at a time. Some of us have detours we can't escape, but like the leaves falling, we gather our strength from You to make sure we will be back again in this great life of family and friends.

Our Father, who art in heaven, hallowed be Thy name. Thy kingdom come. Thy will be done on earth, as it is in heaven. Give us this day our daily bread. And forgive us our debts, as we forgive our debtors. And lead us not into temptation, but deliver us from evil. For Thine is the kingdom, and the power, and the glory, forever. Amen.

FAITH

Dear God,

Taking my hand in Yours, You reestablish my faith whenever I come to You in prayer every day. Time passes so swiftly we have to set a "tempo" for our life. To forget the angry words spoken in haste, help us to share joy and laughter and warmth and love. Life is too short if you're too busy!

Have you ever felt on top of the world? Or gone back to a place you went to as a child? Your heart will smile again by a cheery "hello." Paying your bills. Completing a task you began a long time ago. A note in the mail. A phone call. A noted change can be the spice for life.

Sometimes God answers prayers through someone else. God may choose you as the answer. There are two kinds of hope. The kind you can't do anything about and the kind that you can. Even if the kind you can do something about isn't what you originally wanted, it's still worth doing because a small happiness can make a big sadness less sad.

A rainy day is better than no day! Some dreams do come true so reach out to God when you can't sleep with so many thoughts on your mind. Trust Him.

Our Father, who art in heaven, hallowed be Thy name. Thy kingdom come. Thy will be done on earth, as it is in heaven. Give us this day our daily bread. And forgive us our debts, as we forgive our debtors. And lead us not into temptation, but deliver us from evil. For Thine is the kingdom, and the power, and the glory, forever. Amen.

FAITH

Dear God,

I have had this thought and feeling within me, ever since Crystal shared her "happening" at the prayer chair with me. A young woman sat with her child, who sensed the prayer time and sat so quietly. I know the Holy Spirit was there! It is here within this church. I know that Bob and I were here on a Maundy Thursday service and we both were so touched, we went to the cross that is in our sanctuary and knelt down together and thanked God for touching our lives and hearts.

Prayer is so therapeutic, so personal. It encompasses fear, joy, endurance, a cycle of change, good times, hard times, even war. Listen to your heart! Feel the warmth of the sun on your face or back whenever you can. It's another gift from God.

If you know what you want, try hard to get it. Opportunities will present themselves. Have enthusiasm. Don't do things halfway especially if your childhood lacked in some areas. You can make up for it in later life. A deep appreciation develops for everything. I know. I had to scrub the wood floor every day during the war because at night I had to roll out a piece of canvas to sleep in a corner on the floor with my two younger brothers. This went on for years. It's amazing what you can do when you lose your home and everything. Two beds for six people just doesn't cut it.

I feel truly blessed in my life in this wonderful country named "America." I've learned to do so many things new and different and I thank God for giving me the inner strength to continue in my boundless energy.

Our Father, who art in heaven, hallowed be Thy name. Thy kingdom come. Thy will be done on earth, as it is in heaven. Give us this day our daily bread. And forgive us our debts, as we forgive our debtors. And lead us not into temptation, but deliver us from evil. For Thine is the kingdom, and the power, and the glory, forever. Amen.

FAITH

Dear God,

How wonderful to have our choir members and Karen back from Italy. I'm sure this Vatican trip will go down in their book of memories. Some places and people hold a special place in our hearts. I arrived in America in December 1948. Bob's home in Hanover was beside a huge chicken farm and where they also raised "Great Dane" dogs. I was scared to death of the huge dogs. I also never saw snow or frozen clothes on a "pulley line." The downstairs was heated by an oil stove. The upstairs was unheated including the bathroom. I really thought I was in Siberia. It was freezing!

It was a huge, comical life adjustment for me. I distinctly remember that we didn't complain while living through a war and hoped that some things would change here on Main Street. When life throws you a huge curve, the love of your partner helps you in the adjustment to a new way of life. Do you think we all have a "turning point" in our lives? Learn from your mistakes. Be thankful everyone gets that chance.

Are there some things in life that give you the purest sense of joy? And do you spend a lot of time enjoying it? Each day is a treasure from You, God. Thank You. We live, laugh and play and no matter what has filled our day it's so wonderful to go home. It's a special joy. Believe in yourself and faith in God will get you through your difficult times. I love the everyday "little human things" we encounter that give us happiness.

Embrace music, it will vitalize your inner being and restore your hopes. Children grow up, and we get older. And if we're lucky we'll be blessed to watch and celebrate their lives with a smile. That's a blessing from God.

Our Father, who art in heaven, hallowed be Thy name. Thy kingdom come. Thy will be done on earth, as it is in heaven. Give us this day our daily bread. And forgive us our debts, as we forgive our debtors. And lead us not into temptation, but deliver us from evil. For Thine is the kingdom, and the power, and the glory, forever. Amen.

FAITH

Dear God,

As we age, we realize that we have "special memories" and most of them are happy ones that remain within our hearts and bring a smile to our face. It renews our strength and wisdom to live each day in joy with our own "happy hour!" Feeling loved changes everything. Thank You, God. It's so important to comprehend the how and the why of your life. We all need to create our own recipe of happiness.

Utilize your talents. It is so self-satisfying and it works outwardly to other people with you, widening its circumference. Are your matters of the heart etched completely in your whole being? I hope so! You are blessed. And can you look inwardly at yourself and admit your mistakes to God? We should do that, we would be happier.

Honesty without evasion never takes a back seat. Make every day worthwhile. Love your friends for their true worth. Celebrate precious moments, small miracles and quiet prayers even if you live alone. It's good to travel and do fun things and it's also good to come back knowing you have a home to come back to furnished with love. Always cuddle with your life partner! Do you have a fear of some things? I do. One of mine is "height," so I climb small mountains.

Remember your priorities. Life doesn't always play according to the rules. Sometimes you don't have a choice. It's not easy to accept. Do you think some women are stronger or more resilient than some men? I was the only child in our family sent to English Boarding School. My mother never visited me all those years. I never saw her until I graduated. On reflection, it was a good thing. Other people stepped in to love me and I loved being a part of all those friends. Good things do come out of sad times.

Our Father, who art in heaven, hallowed be Thy name. Thy kingdom come. Thy will be done on earth, as it is in heaven. Give us this day our daily bread. And forgive us our debts, as we forgive our debtors. And lead us not into temptation, but deliver us from evil. For Thine is the kingdom, and the power, and the glory, forever. Amen.

FAITH

Dear God,

It's so amazing how You made bays and inlets, where the ocean is peaceful and calm and on the ocean side the waves and breakers are relentless!!

Are you a morning person or a night person? There are people who are just not "happy people" no matter what their circumstances. Having money and good health doesn't fulfill their persona. Consequently they don't know how to feel grateful and kind or how to savor life, which demands give and take. No one knows you like the people who live with you. No one will care for you the way your family does. A deep bond develops. All the threads in life's experiences eventually get sewn together to make a whole. That gives you the ability to get to the heart of things.

Sometimes a small thing can make you feel so wonderful, and it catches you unawares. Follow your heart. You deserve it. Not all things come your way, fight for what you want. Many moments in your life can become a story, a deep connection. Not knowing what the future holds, you can still feel assured in the deepest part of your heart. If you have God and love in your life, you will feel rich. Take good care of the life partner you love. Closeness comes with familiarity in years.

Have you ever prayed to God to change the course of events happening to you? Try to hold life together even when there's little hope. Sometimes life's lesson is not about holding on, but to let go of the past, so that happiness can complete its full circle. We all need someone to care for and love, that enables us to feel joy. There is no cure for widowhood. Embrace God's love.

Our Father, who art in heaven, hallowed be Thy name. Thy kingdom come. Thy will be done on earth, as it is in heaven. Give us this day our daily bread. And forgive us our debts, as we forgive our debtors. And lead us not into temptation, but deliver us from evil. For Thine is the kingdom, and the power, and the glory, forever. Amen.

FAITH

Dear God,

The world we live in can change so rapidly. Life doesn't come with any guarantees. Is a coincidence just an explanation waiting to happen? It's good to put your life into perspective, rethinking the past. Good memories, disappointments, pride, resentments, forgiveness and also your future. Togetherness, thoughtfulness, love and happiness are a must in any relationship.

Do you analyze the body language and demeanor of a person you're talking to? It's amazing what you can feel and sense! Always make your partner feel important. Your children are part of your life forever and so is a friend you love.

Are you experiencing long, empty days of retirement, or are you pleasantly surprised with so much to do and feeling happy? It's a new life!

The word "cancer" is a fearsome word. It hurts your heart with just the thought of it. It's a terrible moment in your life. Friends are so important, some are the best! Feel their love. It's a gift to you. Be open to attitude adjustments!

Some people are magnets for disaster or have a knack for pushing boundaries to bizarre "what if" moments.

Don't be impervious about your own faults. Do you have a worthy goal in your life? I hope that includes God, prayer, peace and happiness. The sight of a rainbow is God's promise to you.

Our Father, who art in heaven, hallowed be Thy name. Thy kingdom come. Thy will be done on earth, as it is in heaven.

Give us this day our daily bread. And forgive us our debts, as we forgive our debtors. And lead us not into temptation, but deliver us from evil. For Thine is the kingdom, and the power, and the glory, forever. Amen.

FAITH

Dear God,

Nature restores order with our four seasons. Isn't it fun to build a snowman with your children? Take time to be in a quiet place with calm and pleasant thoughts. Celebrate beauty and the renewal of spirit within your whole being.

You can't force someone to feel grateful—it's an inner personal thing. It's hard to believe, but not everyone is kind. Don't excuse a person's faults (like a bad temper) with blindness! Forgive your own sins.

Have you visited a place you took your children to and still enjoyed being there with a past memory? I think people are so interesting. Do you like to study people? There are true friends, kind hearts, worthwhile people nice as pie, and people who have found their niche in life and are excellent in what they do and there are those who think the world owes them a living. It pays to be intuitive and to have a friend with a face you relied on!! You feel their strength and love touching you. That's a special moment! All the tea in China can't replace! I'm glad I'm old enough to realize that! People's demeanor always sends you a message from the way they look at you, or not, and then it's awkward!

Forgiveness is a difficult thing, especially when you can still sense that hurt you've felt—words left said or unsaid. We make mistakes, what counts is how we learn to live with it. Heaviness in your heart can be lifted with God. Silence can sometimes be a kindness and hardships can be a pathway to peace.

Our Father, who art in heaven, hallowed be Thy name. Thy kingdom come. Thy will be done on earth, as it is in heaven. Give us this day our daily bread. And forgive us our debts, as we forgive our debtors. And lead us not into temptation, but deliver us from evil. For Thine is the kingdom, and the power, and the glory, forever. Amen.

FAITH

Dear God,

Prayer is never in vain. Have faith in God. He loves us no matter what. He alone can take that hurt away, especially when there's no way out, he sends a miracle! Never hesitate to fulfill a person's needs, especially a neighbor. This adds to the joy of living. Listen to your heart, no matter what the outcome.

I left a rose at Bob's graveside on November 29th. It was a full moon. We always sat in his truck at Dunkin' Donuts sipping coffee, enjoying the full moon. It was our 65th anniversary. I miss my date! I'm so grateful to have shared 58 years with Bob. He was my rainbow!! So do you have a nightly ritual you treasure? Believe in yourself so that when troubles occur, with faith in God, we will overcome it. Do you have a goal that gets you out of bed? Do your best every day, to plan and see things through, working tenaciously.

Remember to have friendliness and laughter added to the mix. They are gifts we can give to people and to a friend who is always there for you. That person brightens your day, helps you accomplish more than you have ever done before and likes you the way you are. Where there is love, there is a smile and quiet peace. Make this world a better place because of you.

Our Father, who art in heaven, hallowed be Thy name. Thy kingdom come. Thy will be done on earth, as it is in heaven. Give us this day our daily bread. And forgive us our debts, as we forgive our debtors. And lead us not into temptation, but deliver us from evil. For Thine is the kingdom, and the power, and the glory, forever. Amen.

FAITH

Dear God,

I love the quiet, peacefulness of early morning when my thoughts can turn to You with my short and simple prayers. You remind me to take people as they are, to face up to problems, to feel Your love and acceptance for who I am. Don't postpone your happiness and enjoyment until vacation time. Enjoy it now, every day. The "attitude of mind" is the important factor for living a happy life.

I've learned that when your spirit is free, God is so much closer when you make room in your heart for Him. Enjoy humor and laughter. They are important facets to every day. Love your friends for their true worth. Help a child. You will feel renewed. Love changes everything. It creates a soft heart, a cheerful nature.

Make changes if routines become ruts. Look at your self-awareness for the good points and bad. Enjoy the freedom of this wonderful country. Other people have never had that opportunity. This is a time of our life's journey, a time to put our hearts where they belong.

Our Father, who art in heaven, hallowed be Thy name. Thy kingdom come. Thy will be done on earth, as it is in heaven. Give us this day our daily bread. And forgive us our debts, as we forgive our debtors. And lead us not into temptation, but deliver us from evil. For Thine is the kingdom, and the power, and the glory, forever. Amen.

FAITH

Dear God,

Sometimes a problem in your life takes forever to be resolved. You feel as though you're spinning your wheels. You're feeling needy and could use a hug. The problem seems frozen in time, status quo. This is the time for inner strength that defies faith itself, especially when you hear the word *cancer*. It's a challenge to deal with. Think the problem through on the treatment. I know my daughters and I chose the right treatment for me, a commitment that led to longevity for my life that blessed me. Thank You, God!

Some mistakes in life you pay for all your life. Bad things happen to good people. We all carry baggage at some time. Roots don't have to hold you back if you know how to transplant them. Do you feel anchored in your life? Or are you still struggling against the tide? You're never too old to learn something about human nature! Deep in my heart I know I'm an optimistic person and cheerful because I know that God has touched my life. I'm feeling happiness and health from inside out. I want to live long enough to see my children and grandchildren happy, living on life's path with their dreams. Life together is never dull. Alone is a different story. So feel like a part of the family, connected by love.

Be clear about your expectations and emotions. Don't be a bystander. Trust your instincts, be a good parent. Understand your own abilities. It's a vital part of your life if you can laugh in life, you've got it made! Be sure you feel and give love. Have a big heart of thankfulness. It's important to give and take. Pay attention to what makes you feel good, then do it!

Our Father, who art in heaven, hallowed be Thy name. Thy kingdom come. Thy will be done on earth, as it is in heaven. Give us this day our daily bread. And forgive us our debts, as we forgive our debtors. And lead us not into temptation, but deliver us from evil. For Thine is the kingdom, and the power, and the glory, forever. Amen.

FAITH

Dear God,

Isn't it amazing when we see how our children develop some of our traits in the way they deal with their problems at hand? With change comes growth, and when our children are together, to see and feel the love between them, we are blessed!

Life is not just a pathway that leads you on. Take God's hand and follow. Give joy and it will be returned to you within your heart. Be thankful for little things, a hand clasp, a full moon, stars, seeing dimples in a person's face when they smile, a hot bath, and quiet faith.

Memories are important, they come at a moment's call, and they can inspire and console you. Sharing cherished moments with someone special is God's moment for you. Take that time. What your heart loved most is never lost. Strive for simple truths and honest values. Sometimes the best present you can give someone is love, kindness, and thoughtfulness.

I know inner strength is a vital part of the equation. Daily life, responsibilities and dealing with problems motivate you to find your inner healing. You have to ask hard questions of yourself and honestly put the blame where it belongs. Look for parallels of what we create and what is, good points and bad. We mature, circumstances change. We deserve to be happy. So when I feel insecure with an obstacle in my life, I pray. That calms me, renews my faith to hang on in the ever changing sands of time to the cold wash of reality. I know a shattered life can heal because I asked for God's help and I'm standing here praying.

Our Father, who art in heaven, hallowed be Thy name. Thy kingdom come. Thy will be done on earth, as it is in heaven. Give us this day our daily bread. And forgive us our debts, as we forgive our debtors. And lead us not into temptation, but deliver us from evil. For Thine is the kingdom, and the power, and the glory, forever. Amen.

FAITH

Dear God,

One of the most beautiful times of day is early morning when the sun's rays come streaming through the windows, throwing light on everything. You feel like you're on Cloud 9 feeling a centered spirit, being in the right place at the right time. Sometimes your heart can be far away on a special person.

Do you believe in a divine plan with a good ending? We need wisdom to know what's important to us to be better people in life. We all need a guardian angel to get us through our happenings. It's always sad to say good bye to a loved one, but it's much sadder when you know you'll never see them again. I've learned that with God, you can focus on the major issues and let the small issues fall into place. You make choices and when you decide to do something, you better love it. It's worth the effort.

Having children changes you, inside and out! You watch sunsets, feed the birds, read to them and play games like "One, Two, Three, Red Light!" You feel grateful and happy, loved and needed. We need gentle contact. We can always learn to respect our different values and differences.

Appreciate your talents, build trust. Don't take things for granted. We all have dreams, ambitions and choices. We shape our own destiny and we are all on borrowed time. We can't turn back the clock and if you try it's often disappointing. Life isn't always fair. Sometimes we don't know what we have until we lose it. Everyone has a chance to let go of the past or make up for it. With a leap of faith and hope for the best it's possible.

Our Father, who art in heaven, hallowed be Thy name. Thy kingdom come. Thy will be done on earth, as it is in heaven. Give us this day our daily bread. And forgive us our debts, as we forgive our debtors. And lead us not into temptation, but deliver us from evil. For Thine is the kingdom, and the power, and the glory, forever. Amen.

FAITH

Dear God,

The horror of war makes you brave one minute and a coward in the next. I remember 1945 when American troops freed us. We were alive! We had food again, power and water, hot water especially. We were able to feel safe on the streets and live without fear. We spent a lot of time working ourselves into a feeling of being all right again, re-evaluating our lives. It was time for a good attitude, for change and broadening our lives. There's always the right thing to do at the right time.

Be a survivor—embrace joy—in spite of witnessing the worst human behavior. The best things in life are not just free, but unexpected. Some people are lucky in life and love! We always turn to God in prayer when trouble surrounds us; likewise we should turn to Him when we are at peace.

Have you ever met a person coming from a different starting point and ended up finding out that their thoughts were similar to yours? Adversity builds character. We need challenges, we need togetherness. Not everything is as it seems. People react to things in different ways. Some people spread sunshine and warmth and some spread other signals.

Take control and try to be positive and productive with less trouble and sorrow. Let the Holy Spirit move you within the central core of your being. Be a listener and supporter of enthusiasm for life. Compliment something in a person. If we're lucky, we will meet someone who is like a "Guardian Angel" who will give us hope to continue to live with a smile.

Our Father, who art in heaven, hallowed be Thy name. Thy kingdom come. Thy will be done on earth, as it is in heaven. Give us this day our daily bread. And forgive us our debts, as we forgive our debtors. And lead us not into temptation, but deliver us from evil. For Thine is the kingdom, and the power, and the glory, forever. Amen.

FAITH

Dear God,

Many times people at an older age harness a talent that has been dormant for years. It's amazing how much joy that can instill in your life. Happiness is an overwhelming feeling!! A lifetime of controlled energy, radiating though you. Self-esteem is so important and in order to have it, you must believe in yourself first. Life can bring complete joy or misery. There's always a turning point in spite of failure or mistakes.

Lean on God. Yesterdays have to be faced in order to move forward. Do you conceal your thoughts easily? Do you show your feelings with a frown or smile? There's a whole lot to understanding the difference in working alongside someone instead of working for someone. Some people stay the same, some change. Every choice a person makes takes them somewhere. Focus on the moment, enjoy it, live it. Business is business. Life is life!! It depends on how you look at it.

Trade your job for freedom—call it "retirement!" Time is your own. It's your time to shine. Do something different and pleasant. Do you feel discrimination against something? Bob's mother didn't accept or like me because I was a "foreigner," a Catholic, and wasn't white with blue eyes. That was a difficult hurt. Bob was horrified and suffered through a separation with his mother. She never had a change of heart to reconcile the differences. There is living after change and hurt with God's help and timeless grace. It was so wonderful to have someone like Bob who loved me and made me feel safe and comforted and happy. That kind of memory lives forever, untouched by time.

Our Father, who art in heaven, hallowed be Thy name. Thy kingdom come. Thy will be done on earth, as it is in heaven. Give us this day our daily bread. And forgive us our debts, as we forgive our debtors. And lead us not into temptation, but deliver us from evil. For Thine is the kingdom, and the power, and the glory, forever. Amen.

FAITH

Dear God,

You alone know what's best for me, and the way I must live my life. I feel such peace taking Your hand with love in promise for another new day. Thank You. The honesties of life we all face, be it heartache or joy, remind us of You!! That makes each one of us feel special.

To have music in our lives is a huge dimension of pleasure, faith, and joy. We need that bonding together. Life is a pattern. Which one of you is creating? I hope you'll select love, friendship, thoughtfulness, faith, and happiness. Thank You, God, for your example.

Our family is a gift from You. We provide the values of love and trust to them from You, God. We should live to learn and be happy with laughter and smiles for tomorrow is always a mystery. Have you ever enjoyed the precious peace and quiet of an early morning? It's so-o-o good for your soul. There are times in your life with friends when no words need to be spoken, they are simply felt.

Have you ever had something traumatic happen to you that's etched in your psyche? I'm sure we all have within our lifetime. It's so important how you deal with it. Life is too worthwhile to feel used and necessary, instead of loved through the years. It's sad to realize things in life too late to correct them. Living alone is another whole ball game. Reach out in love, a day at a time as we travel life's pathway simply and truthfully. You will feel blessed.

Do you think there are many kinds of love people have a capacity for? I do. Think about it. Even in your home, isn't there a certain room that you just love to be in? Your feelings change within it. Our own peaceful sanctuary! Listen to your heart. Do what makes you happy.

Our Father, who art in heaven, hallowed be Thy name. Thy kingdom come. Thy will be done on earth, as it is in heaven. Give us this day our daily bread. And forgive us our debts, as we forgive our debtors. And lead us not into temptation, but deliver us from evil. For Thine is the kingdom, and the power, and the glory, forever. Amen.

FAITH

Dear God,

Thank You for our four seasons because each season is a "masterpiece." We have the gift of spring fragrance, summer sunsets, fall leaves of splendor, and winter's snow as a promise.

How many would give anything in the world to be held by the one person they love? I feel that even though Bob has passed, I see his face in anyone I love. He will always be there for me. Sorrow gives way to peace. Keep something of the one you love like a talisman, touching or looking at it sometimes. That is a moment of grace, a memory that all has not been lost.

Enjoy the smell of coffee, bacon frying, and a restful night's sleep. God's gift to you is your family. Enjoy the relationship because the game's not over, especially with grandchildren. They keep us young and remind us that there's still a lot of happy living to do.

In Chinese the word "crisis" is the same word as "opportunity." Think about it. At times we need our spirit to be rekindled by someone else, especially a grandchild. It's wonderful to be in a home where families live and love abounds. Giving of yourself just by listening to someone with a hurting heart, you restore their hope by your caring. It gives purpose to your life and joy to your heart.

Feel God's love day after day, recalling His goodness and blessing in your life. Thank Him.

Our Father, who art in heaven, hallowed be Thy name. Thy kingdom come. Thy will be done on earth, as it is in heaven.

Give us this day our daily bread. And forgive us our debts, as we forgive our debtors. And lead us not into temptation, but deliver us from evil. For Thine is the kingdom, and the power, and the glory, forever. Amen.

FAITH

Dear God,

Every morning You paint a new picture. Fall, with colorful leaves bursting in beauty is a gift from You reminding us that a heart that is glad is a heart that is free! As summer retreats, autumn brings new gladness and joy. Apple picking, pumpkins, chrysanthemums, crispness in the air bring us a new vitality! We all need to recharge our batteries at times.

Pay attention to your gut feelings on decisions concerning health, career, and education. It's just as important as your mind needs to shut off and relax and not be like a beaver taking down a tree. It's a good adjustment to try. All my life I've had a surplus of energy, but I know when I run on empty.

You can be organized, but not predictable. Accept yourself. We need fun and we need quiet solace, too. It's difficult not to get emotional when dealing with "family" issues, and to remain level-headed instead of over-reacting. So, if you really look at your life, you'll discover many things and tricks "fate" can play on us. Simple truths and honest values are ageless. Don't have a blind spot in your heart!

God knows you, and loves you. We need to be our own person, if we don't, our life will feel empty inside of us. There are so many good people in this world savoring "kindness" every day. So put your hand into the hand of God, it will fill your whole being.

Our Father, who art in heaven, hallowed be Thy name. Thy kingdom come. Thy will be done on earth, as it is in heaven. Give us this day our daily bread. And forgive us our debts, as we

forgive our debtors. And lead us not into temptation, but deliver us from evil. For Thine is the kingdom, and the power, and the glory, forever. Amen.

FAITH

Dear God,

Thank You for the seasons that remind us of all the beauty around us. You created it!! You love us and show Your caring for us in every way. If we feel sad and turn to You, You touch our hearts with that feeling of "love-beam" that lets us know You are on that journey with us.

Likewise in happy times, that "warm-beam" feeling of joy that fills my being is another gift from You. You show us that through sorrow, there is tenderness and richness to live a life that counts.

There is nothing that You cannot heal in our pathway of life. I totally trust You!! We all lose precious people or things in our life, but there is one thing that remains steadfast and true: it is You, God.

In prayer You have comforted me through hours of hunger, fear, and sorrow. On a daily basis my strength is renewed. We need to hold Your hand for that comfort that calms us with Your spirit. You alone listen to all that we think, say and do. Thank You for my life that always puts a smile on my face.

Our Father, who art in heaven, hallowed be Thy name. Thy kingdom come. Thy will be done on earth, as it is in heaven. Give us this day our daily bread. And forgive us our debts, as we forgive our debtors. And lead us not into temptation, but deliver us from evil. For Thine is the kingdom, and the power, and the glory, forever. Amen.

FAITH

Dear God,

Life is the first gift. Love is second. Understanding is the third. Aging gives us acquired understanding. We have life's experiences to draw and sustain us in wisdom. The paradox of the kingdom of God is through defeat of a cross. God is glorified! Healing happens through brokenness, by finding yourself. I'm sure that love continues beyond loss. Never lose faith. Know where you belong. That is true comfort by the grace of God.

Trouble shared is trouble halved! Learn the wisdom of compromise—it's better to bond than to break. Give with your whole heart because a lifetime is specializing in alterations. The greater part of our happiness or misery depends on our dispositions. The price to gain peace demands courage.

Happiness turns up to a woman sweeping her driveway, painting a picket fence, knitting or crocheting. Happiness turns up in a sun rising and a moon shining; happiness turns up for your family and loved ones. So look for joy instead of sorrow. Nobody has measured how much the heart can hold.

Trust God, feel His love, you are never alone. The Holy Spirit is here. We grow from inside ourselves to outwardly feeling and reaching out to each other. Faith is a state of mind that grows out of our actions just as it also governs them. Think about learning to swim or how to ride a bike; learn a new language. Isn't it amazing what we can accomplish in this journey of life! So feel the pleasure for these moments.

Our Father, who art in heaven, hallowed be Thy name. Thy kingdom come. Thy will be done on earth, as it is in heaven. Give us this day our daily bread. And forgive us our debts, as we forgive our debtors. And lead us not into temptation, but deliver us from evil. For Thine is the kingdom, and the power, and the glory, forever. Amen.

FAITH

Dear God,

I so love and enjoy a sunny day in winter! It's a reminder that spring is coming soon. Footprints of creatures and people in the snow will disappear. Do you think people who think small usually end up with small lives? Does the world work that way or can we change that? Know your place in life and be true to it.

Some things are part of our daily life for months and then they are gone just like that! If you are burdened with heavy news and feel sad and dispirited, try to smile in spite of a brutal day. You can be in good spirits when the odds are stacked. There's still a realm of possibility to conquer it. Life is a mixture of happiness, sorrow and pain.

We are all given wisdom to unfold in our life—moment to moment to enjoy happiness, love and a thankful heart. Take time to say "I love you." We get so busy we neglect those we love the most and persons we keep close within our heart. Never lose faith and trust in God. He's always there to hold your hand and give you peace of mind. That is your moment with God. Inspire your heart. Walk in happiness each day. Be thankful for little things that we see and feel—a smile, a visit with a friend, a walk with your grandchild.

These are the things that bind us and make us who we are today. Be gracious. Sooner is always better than later. Enjoy children, each child is so amazing. I love children; they bring so much joy.

Our Father, who art in heaven, hallowed be Thy name. Thy kingdom come. Thy will be done on earth, as it is in heaven.

Give us this day our daily bread. And forgive us our debts, as we forgive our debtors. And lead us not into temptation, but deliver us from evil. For Thine is the kingdom, and the power, and the glory, forever. Amen.

FAITH

Dear God,

My thoughts are all about Christmas, Your Son's birthday. I love the story in the bible that tells about Mary and how You came to Joseph and told him to marry her and name the baby Jesus and that He would do wonders in the world. I'm convinced that what I lacked in my life has come full circle now. Thank You, God.

Bob got me my first Christmas tree here in America. I'd never had one before in my life. I'm sure that's one of the reasons I love Christmas. It's not just a holiday, it's a miracle with so much meaning within me. It's a personal occasion.

Have you ever felt God's presence in your life? I have many times. Sometimes we have to start over with a new life to feel vindicated and happy again. That's an important criterion for you. It makes your heart sing again. I hope your life isn't like a boat drifting, going nowhere with no hope of getting anywhere.

In relationships there has to be teamwork and understanding as well as recognizing each other's needs and love. Take time to look at the moon and stars, it'll do wonders for your soul. Happiness doesn't come only to the beautiful and handsome.

Are you a person always doing the right thing at the right time? Through heartaches you can pick up the pieces, so celebrate your life for yourself, your children, good health, friends, and love. Move forward, it's your bonus from God. Be willing to change some things. We all make mistakes. Forgive yourself. Remember Christmas is love and the treasures in your life are not just the gifts, but simply the feeling of love for one another.

120

Our Father, who art in heaven, hallowed be Thy name. Thy kingdom come. Thy will be done on earth, as it is in heaven. Give us this day our daily bread. And forgive us our debts, as we forgive our debtors. And lead us not into temptation, but deliver us from evil. For Thine is the kingdom, and the power, and the glory, forever. Amen.

FAITH

Dear God,

Marathon Monday, April 15th, 2013!! How tragic, how sad that there were people around who wanted to hurt and kill other people. The saddest people in life are persons who don't care deeply. Our world is turned upside down. Think of the Richards family of Dorchester. Their eight-year-old son killed, Mom's brain was injured, their daughter lost limbs, and they had come to cheer Dad. Only he and one older son in fifth grade remain physically whole but scarred with unbelievable emotional tragedy.

We all need someone to share sad news with when it arrives. It can age a person depending on the depth of grief! It's difficult to lose someone you love. It can be an eternity missing that person. Efforts to help someone can fail miserably at times, but true love exists even in the darkest hours. Take time for quiet moments. Be glad you're alive and well. When horrible things happen in your life, try to think about someone who is a blessing you. Turn to God. He will help you heal and even when you think that happiness is as distant as space travel.

This marathon has put us on an emotional roller coaster. It's upsetting and terrifying. We need a vote of confidence in spirit, we need to feel that the guilty will be found and punished. We need a surge of hope that touches our hearts. We know fate is unpredictable; however, in this situation we need to feel closure to this chapter so that there's a chance to enjoy life again.

So reach out to God with love and trust. He will renew your spirit to continue in life.

Our Father, who art in heaven, hallowed be Thy name. Thy kingdom come. Thy will be done on earth, as it is in heaven. Give us this day our daily bread. And forgive us our debts, as we forgive our debtors. And lead us not into temptation, but deliver us from evil. For Thine is the kingdom, and the power, and the glory, forever. Amen.

FAITH

Dear God,

I love my quiet times with You when I can put my thoughts together. You've always helped me through trying times. I know Your promise to us is Your grace and strength for each hurt we go through, with love, peace and forgiveness. Thank You for Your loving care—what a gift!

Today my thoughts are with my only sister. For years I still keep writing and remembering her birthday. I give her compliments on all her attributes and talent, and tell her I love her, but she remains steadfast in her desire to slot out the family as she doesn't want to remember Shanghai, China. I respect her wishes so I have not seen her forever.

Distance can do strange things to people. She has not allowed her three sons to be in touch also. Disappointing, yes, so I try to focus on joy, my grandchildren and friends and my one remaining brother and keep memories alive in my heart of her and her family.

Comfort can be found in the steady routines of life. I know as my children age they will always remember the things I've said to them and what I did with them. We teach them values. Don't give up the little things that make life worthwhile. We all want peace in our hearts; life without too many disappointments. Knowing you are a worthy human being your confidence grows and you become stronger.

Do you accomplish just about everything you set out to do? Running is like a form of meditation, when you're alone doing it. We all live in a world with limitations that don't allow us to live in the moment. That's not always fair! Sometimes we need to change the rules to become a better person than we had been. That takes courage.

Our Father, who art in heaven, hallowed be Thy name. Thy kingdom come. Thy will be done on earth, as it is in heaven. Give us this day our daily bread. And forgive us our debts, as we forgive our debtors. And lead us not into temptation, but deliver us from evil. For Thine is the kingdom, and the power, and the glory, forever. Amen.

MUSIC

Dear God,

This year during Lent, Karen's "Musical Meditations" have made this time so much more meaningful! I have always felt it was a time to look inward in thought to our low or high areas, to be honest in admissions and to seek to do better. Different people touch us in so many ways, always with Your grace and kindness.

This choir in particular is such a group. They take Your love and channel it out in so many ways. That is such a blessing that not everyone in life experiences. They, as individuals, reflect their love for You by their thoughts, their actions and beliefs.

All this creates the beautiful music we can sing about and perhaps touch a person's heart and inward spirit.

What would we do without music in our lives?

What would we do and be without God in our lives?

So I thank Karen, the choir, the church and each one of you here. You are the other half of my rainbow!!

Let us pray.

Our Father, who art in heaven, hallowed be Thy name. Thy kingdom come. Thy will be done on earth, as it is in heaven. Give us this day our daily bread. And forgive us our debts, as we forgive our debtors. And lead us not into temptation, but deliver us from evil. For Thine is the kingdom, and the power, and the glory, forever. Amen.

MUSIC

Dear God,

We are so lucky to have Karen as our Music Minister! Another awesome concert! It was a happy, joyful feeling with the audience and within us! Each one of us in this choir is one of God's angels. The depth of love and caring is incredible. The message you send out is not only in music but also one of God's love within us. Thank You for letting me be a part of it.

What you accomplish in life is never more valuable than the person you are. The word "us" is a very small word, but if you own it, you're a winner! With music in our lives, life is never that bad. It gives you a feeling of happiness and appreciation for another person. That's a blessing. Moment to moment, when we just give music, we feel in a different state of mind.

Your job or career isn't just "work" if you're doing what you love to do. Admit your truths to yourself and share it with God. Sometimes we kid ourselves about so much time to do this and that. Truthfully, life, love, and loss happen so often. Don't let family pressures be more important than what is in your heart. Love yourself. It's so great to have someone beside you to share everything.

Do you like your life? We learn to make a new and different life after a loss or divorce to feel happiness and love again. Dare to hope, dare to dream, God is there for you. Say "Merry Christmas" to each of us. I can't believe I'm in the midst of the most wonderful people who live each day with love, thoughtfulness, kindness and talent. God is smiling and so is my heart.

Our Father, who art in heaven, hallowed be Thy name. Thy kingdom come. Thy will be done on earth, as it is in heaven. Give us this day our daily bread. And forgive us our debts, as we forgive our debtors. And lead us not into temptation, but deliver us from evil. For Thine is the kingdom, and the power, and the glory, forever. Amen.

MUSIC

Dear God,

It is in quiet times of prayer when we can feel the joy of knowing You, feeling your smile. You bless us in so many ways every day with love, laughter, music and song. Hearing Karen play for the Lenten Meditations restores our being.

I love being alive to experience it all. We need to take the time to thank You for everything. We shouldn't miss the simple things: a moment, a rainbow, a smile, a child's first step, a flower's bloom, colored leaves and snow.

God, You are always there when we're troubled, or when our spirits are low. You hear our confessions and confidences and continually give us the new strength to face life's daily tasks.

It is so peaceful to know that we have You as our refuge. We are reminded to keep looking up! The choices we make, the give and take—it's all part of living. With You in our lives, life is a treasure we can possess and know that we are loved.

Our Father, who art in heaven, hallowed be Thy name. Thy kingdom come. Thy will be done on earth, as it is in heaven. Give us this day our daily bread. And forgive us our debts, as we forgive our debtors. And lead us not into temptation, but deliver us from evil. For Thine is the kingdom, and the power, and the glory, forever. Amen.

MUSIC

Dear God,

I want to thank You for my friends. They touch my life with love. I know I can pour out the contents of my heart to them, knowing that the gentlest hands will take and sift my thoughts, keeping what is worthy and with kindness, throwing away the rest.

This is the time for taxes. Don't you feel like a million after you pay them? In the game of life, do you step up to the plate? As a woman, I loved being married to a man who centered on me and the children.

Family is a gift from You, God. Only You can give us that special peace within our hearts. You look down and send us the sun, smooth our pathways and dry our tears. Each day is a treasure! All You ask in return is our love.

Thank You for the musical experience we had sharing with other churches. For me it made me so aware of this wonderful group of people in this choir. Karen is our gift from God. She keeps challenging us towards singing better, with expression and vowels and to look up at her. She is truly our star! We awed the other choirs with our bell choir. They heard music from the heavens.

The purpose of life is the expansion of happiness and music is certainly an important component towards it. Your mind and body's reaction to music is joy filling your being, mentally and physically.

Our Father, who art in heaven, hallowed be Thy name. Thy kingdom come. Thy will be done on earth, as it is in heaven. Give us this day our daily bread. And forgive us our debts, as we forgive our debtors. And lead us not into temptation, but deliver us from evil. For Thine is the kingdom, and the power, and the glory, forever. Amen.

MUSIC

Dear God,

For some reason this Easter service was so uplifting for me!!
The musicians, soloist, the choir singing floor level instead of
being just "loft people," having fun with "Domine Fili," listening
to and watching the bells—hours of learning, grooming and
smoothing that art form. I loved watching Karen, as director, for
rhythm and personality and talent. It truly restored belief in God.
The music in this church is the best on the South Shore!! Thank
you, Karen! Thank you, choir! I was left with a rush of
adrenaline for the whole day.

Spring is a time for new beginnings. Pay tribute to someone or
something. Have lovely memories that are stored in your heart.
Strive to bring happiness to people you touch in your life. You
will feel joy in simple things, a baby's smile, your grandchildren,
and your family. Enjoy the love surrounding you. It's a gift
from God.

Time has a way of dimming the edges of reality. No matter how
often we stumble in life, God is always there to lift us up, time
after time. Is there a reason when certain people come into your
life? Think about it! Sometimes waiting for something to
happen can seem like an eternity. Be aware of an opportunity
when presented, don't ignore it. Know what you want out of this
life. Be comfortable with your choice, be responsible. Be gung
ho about something!

Value nature, beauty and peacefulness, and love the spectacular
vistas up in the mountains. Feel your wellbeing in a place. Feel
the generosity of time and love of a friend that touches your
heart.

Our Father, who art in heaven, hallowed be Thy name. Thy kingdom come. Thy will be done on earth, as it is in heaven. Give us this day our daily bread. And forgive us our debts, as we forgive our debtors. And lead us not into temptation, but deliver us from evil. For Thine is the kingdom, and the power, and the glory, forever. Amen.

MUSIC

Dear God,

Thank You for a joyful Easter of family and friends and togetherness. It truly is a special feeling. It reminds us that after sorrow, there can be happiness. Think of the shape of a triangle representing parents and children and feel the feeling of protection and love for your children forever, no matter the age.

Do you have something all-encompassing in your life? Karen comes to my mind as "music" obviously. All of us here love music and singing, it's part of our soul. As you age, do you think you're wiser? Or do you feel you're losing ground? Miracles do happen that can change you inside out. Don't believe only in the here, now and visible. We all have family and friends who love us! It doesn't get better than that!!

Have you ever had someone look at you in a long, steady, direct way, and feel they could see inside you to your heart? Savor it! Learn from all you do each day with patience, humor, and kindness, and it will reflect your joy in your eyes. A sensing heart always knows the way to our greatest happiness. You are the creator of its journey.

I love how when you love a friend or family member and you don't see them face-to-face for ages, you know their love remains, no matter what. Love is a gift from God. Love can hurt, but it can also heal. Have you ever thought about that when a person believes in you? It gives you the strength to do anything. You're not alone. We also need that love to move forward with belief in ourselves.

Remember that unconditional love you feel for your children? Do you have a person who has been a unique influence in your life? That's special, especially when there is an unspoken understanding between you. Sometimes we spend a lifetime trying to belong somewhere, forgetting God is in our corner. Take His hand.

Our Father, who art in heaven, hallowed be Thy name. Thy kingdom come. Thy will be done on earth, as it is in heaven. Give us this day our daily bread. And forgive us our debts, as we forgive our debtors. And lead us not into temptation, but deliver us from evil. For Thine is the kingdom, and the power, and the glory, forever. Amen.

MUSIC

Dear God,

Here we are again, our first choir rehearsal in September 2013. It's exciting because this circle of people gather with love for each other and love for You. With Karen, our beautiful leader, we will sing from our hearts in thankfulness to You.

I hope you all had a good summer and feel that life is good when walking the beach, or watching the ocean with waves rolling and curling in a dance, with bubbles hitting the beach. Every day is a gift from God.

Being missed by someone is another blessing. A gesture like a hug can touch your heart!! Do you have a favorite time of day you love? Mine is the morning! A great life partner makes bad times bearable, and good times magical!

Memories are a part of you that no one can take away. Have a zest for life! Keeping busy has curative powers, it benefits you more than being at a standstill. You can have a job, but do you do it with warmth and enthusiasm? Without those ingredients it can get very matter-of-fact.

Sometimes an adventure with something is a good thing or a challenge. There are errands of kindness we have to do at times, and they stay with you for life. Be close with some people, be a good ambassador in your life and job. Have the capacity to understand. Always go for a walk when you're upset and talk to God.

Our Father, who art in heaven, hallowed be Thy name. Thy kingdom come. Thy will be done on earth, as it is in heaven.

Give us this day our daily bread. And forgive us our debts, as we forgive our debtors. And lead us not into temptation, but deliver us from evil. For Thine is the kingdom, and the power, and the glory, forever. Amen.

MUSIC

Dear God,

This was the most snow I've seen in many years! I stay put because You know how I seriously have a hard time backing up in my driveway on a good day!!

Do you plan every aspect of your life because your mind just won't shut off? Or do you want what you have now? Simple truths and honest values are ageless. On any day, remember flowers are like "soul food" for the heart! Bob gave flowers "just because." Wake up to a whole new day with happiness and thank God. Have and do things in your life that have meaning, be generous with praise, and be passionate.

We all have burdens we wish we could undo. Life is a gamble at times, but if you have a friend you grew up with, went to school with, they become a part of your family. Those friendships are a blessing. Know what is important to you. Like yourself! A sign of a good executive is a good staff. Use good earthy common sense in decisions. Love your family.

Life isn't fair and never promises to be. Be spontaneous in what you do because parenting and worrying are synonymous. Be aware—feel and sense when coincidences have a meaning. Do fun things because later in life you will remember them and feel free and alive—inside and out! Be glad God is in your life. Never break a promise when you give one. Have thoughtful insights, handle whatever comes along, enjoy and appreciate your area of living.

Have you ever been in a place that gave you a feeling of serenity? I have one of the places right here, when Karen plays her music during meditations.

Our Father, who art in heaven, hallowed be Thy name. Thy kingdom come. Thy will be done on earth, as it is in heaven. Give us this day our daily bread. And forgive us our debts, as we forgive our debtors. And lead us not into temptation, but deliver us from evil. For Thine is the kingdom, and the power, and the glory, forever. Amen.

MUSIC

Dear God,

Thank You for the promise of a new day! For each and every one of us this day is another chance at happiness and peace of mind and to reflect on our life. Today, we celebrate Karen's birthday! It is so special because You blessed her with an awesome talent of music. This church would not be that spectacular without her! Our lives are enriched as well as hers by her leadership and effort.

Music fills our souls, and without music in our lives we would not experience the utter joy it brings. So, thank you, Karen, we love you. Thank you for touching our lives and for being you. You make us smile.

Treat people thoughtfully because it makes you a stronger, better person. Appreciate the good things that happen to you, love what you do and be true to yourself. Happiness is being aware of how lucky you are to have the people you have around you and your health. Human instinct makes us feel the need for safety and security. Learn to compromise and change. Feel the liberating, peaceful journey that holds you together. Be truthful and apologize if you need to.

Do you ever feel overwhelmed by something? We all need a glimmer of hope to carry on. There is no right age to accomplish something and try a new endeavor. Think of Nancy who is learning to ring bells! Be your own person. Have God's spirit within you.

Do you have something that drives you daily to get out of bed? We need that impulse. Life is good. Make your life interesting.

Honor yourself, you're special. Make God smile. Being born in Shanghai, China doesn't take away my feeling of "home" here in America. Honestly, for me there are no more "fixed bayonets" and hunger. I went down to 87 pounds. America, for me, is you, the people that give it the magic.

Our Father, who art in heaven, hallowed be Thy name. Thy kingdom come. Thy will be done on earth, as it is in heaven. Give us this day our daily bread. And forgive us our debts, as we forgive our debtors. And lead us not into temptation, but deliver us from evil. For Thine is the kingdom, and the power, and the glory, forever. Amen.

MUSIC

Dear God,

Thank You for Karen and this extraordinary group of people. Under her leadership we learn and sing to Your glory! We all love music. It renews our very being. It puts joy in our lives. This choir is a bright light to what You mean in our various lives. Each choir member's thoughts and kind deeds are always in motion.

I am so blessed to be amongst them. Truly the Holy Spirit is here. Each one has had their share of burdens and happiness, but we carry on because we have You to turn to. That alone is the comfort we need. There is no time like the present to sing, to enjoy a vacation, to hug a grandchild, lunch with a friend or enjoy your garden.

Do what you can for others because a heart that's happy is a heart that is free. It's also a great feeling to come home and have a quiet, happy heart.

Live and love, be a heart of kindness, fulfill a neighbor's need. Don't let troubles of life get you down. With God's help there is peace. Trust Him. He will never let you down. He is the light at the end of the tunnel. We don't know the window of tomorrow, so live each day's precious moments. For each day is a blessing.

Our Father, who art in heaven, hallowed be Thy name. Thy kingdom come. Thy will be done on earth, as it is in heaven. Give us this day our daily bread. And forgive us our debts, as we forgive our debtors. And lead us not into temptation, but deliver us from evil. For Thine is the kingdom, and the power, and the glory, forever. Amen.

MUSIC

Dear God,

Thanksgiving! I really never heard about it until the American forces freed us. Now I love the tradition of families and friends gathering together for roast turkey and all the fixings. Feeling good inwardly and out! It's a happy occasion. We have so much to be thankful for. I know that only God could have touched my life to make it into what it is.

It is a blessing to be here in America living without fear, having abundant food and enjoying good health. To have been married to Bob for 58 years and to have my family and grandchildren, I am grateful. I love my beautiful, warm home because Bob was born here and that's very special. I feel Bob's spirit every day. I am thankful for the wonderful friends I have.

This choir is made up of people living and radiating God's love. With Karen as our leader, who composes beautiful music from her heart and mind, we sing tribute to You, God. This choir is full of angels with music in our souls, gratefully singing praise to You, God, and sharing the feelings of our whole being with others. That's a good life. We all need music in it to make us happy!

Thanksgiving to me is like a beautiful tapestry with thousands of pieces of thread in all colors being woven in with love, friendship, kindness and thoughtfulness. No money could ever purchase this tapestry—its value in worth is happiness in our inner being and core of feelings. So on this holiday, look inwardly at yourself and thank God for all you have.

Our Father, who art in heaven, hallowed be Thy name. Thy kingdom come. Thy will be done on earth, as it is in heaven. Give us this day our daily bread. And forgive us our debts, as we forgive our debtors. And lead us not into temptation, but deliver us from evil. For Thine is the kingdom, and the power, and the glory, forever. Amen.

TRUST AND COMFORT

Dear God,

It's perfectly natural to grieve over the loss of your pet, be it a dog or a cat. They are our extended family. So it's a teary, sad time that my neighbor just got through. She is healing with time and good memories. We all need someone to love and have our love returned. Have you ever gotten so excited when buying a gift for someone special imagining the look of happiness on their face? That's when love is a many splendored thing. Pick a right time. Everyone has their own pain and happiness, but can you ever get over the death of a child? That's huge. To get to a place of peace of mind and joy again, lean on God and feel that you can open up your heart to Him and let it all go.

Different isn't a bad thing. Face the truth. It brings peace in your life and helps you stay the course. We all need to be comforted at times. Does age make a traumatic difference to accept and deal with a problem? Thank God for music. It always makes you feel better, no matter what. We leave one life to lead another one realizing what works for you. That's a good thing.

Different temperaments, levels of patience, and hope all make up your daily life. So are you a person who either snaps at people or strokes gently instead? Wrong decisions have to be cleaned up in order to be happy. Don't be an escape artist. We need to step back and see what we've accomplished instead. Enjoy curiosity and wonder. It keeps you young.

Appreciate what you have and age gracefully even though the clock keeps ticking. Remember the sun rises every day, and each day is our very own. Thank God for His beautiful rainbows. Home is where we find joy, a smile, and love. It's a place where our hearts can rest, and where you can be the person you want to be. It makes life worthwhile.

Our Father, who art in heaven, hallowed be Thy name. Thy kingdom come. Thy will be done on earth, as it is in heaven. Give us this day our daily bread. And forgive us our debts, as we forgive our debtors. And lead us not into temptation, but deliver us from evil. For Thine is the kingdom, and the power, and the glory, forever. Amen.

TRUST AND COMFORT

Dear God,

Divorce or death in real life is a huge drama. However, with belief in yourself and God, you can achieve quality of life and happiness again. The love surrounding you by family and friends adds to that triumph. Live life. It's God's gift to you. Use it happily every day. It works. I promise you. When something great happens in your life, feel it and enjoy it! There is no excuse for ugly behavior. Life is not necessarily fair. Minimize your life if you have to. Allow yourself a break. Even as a mother, don't be a martyr 24/7.

Some people are leaders. I'm a follower in the "happy to help category." There are no guarantees on most things, least of all your future. So when facing trauma, we either cry and dissolve into a puddle or take the blow and face it to make it bearable. Know yourself, pay attention to your inner heart. Maybe who we are isn't as important as what we do or can do when we least expect it. We realize that we don't always get what we think we deserve. Do you have someone in your life who disappoints you regularly? The answer is to have fewer expectations from that person because it makes it easier for you to deal with that individual.

When you love someone, you love them in spite of imperfections. Have you ever thought about your friends who have been in your life forever? They give you hope, love, kindness, and faithfulness. They listen, feel your happenings, and help you move on. They reenergize and cheer you. Friends help friends, and you feel the world is a better place. Age gives us a chance to make good things, great things day-to-day. Celebrate being alive. Your disposition alone affects your health. There are so many good people in this world who can touch your heart.

Our Father, who art in heaven, hallowed be Thy name. Thy kingdom come. Thy will be done on earth, as it is in heaven. Give us this day our daily bread. And forgive us our debts, as we forgive our debtors. And lead us not into temptation, but deliver us from evil. For Thine is the kingdom, and the power, and the glory, forever. Amen.

TRUST AND COMFORT

Dear God,

Summertime is flying by, Bob's sister died. Judy, a best friend of mine, also died. Loss brings pain, but it also triggers memories that will comfort a rise within each one of us by the grace of God. He will wipe every tear from your eye, and He will change your pain to laughter with His tender power. There is no accounting for happiness or the way it turns up—a special song, good news, a full moon, a good check-up at the doctors, and feeling loved! Life goes by so quickly, so make another person happy, and you will be happy, too! How we live is what counts.

Why do some people treat strangers better than their own family? Because love from family and friends is a huge treasure. Wrong words can hurt. Have you ever stayed in a job even though the salary wasn't great simply because you were happy in it? Sometimes it's good to follow your heart. If you have someone you love beside you, in any situation, you can deal with it so much easier. Give a hug. Sharing your life is as good as it gets.

You don't need a special occasion to celebrate. Spur of the moment ideas do wonders for your soul. Make your life meaningful, know and realize the inner spirit of yourself and feel that joy. The older you get, you know that putting up with the good and bad is all a part of love. Say "I love you" and mean it! People living without love carry an emptiness within them. Do you think that the truest measure of a person is in what they love? Open your heart, love God.

Our Father, who art in heaven, hallowed be Thy name. Thy kingdom come. Thy will be done on earth, as it is in heaven. Give us this day our daily bread. And forgive us our debts, as we

149

forgive our debtors. And lead us not into temptation, but deliver us from evil. For Thine is the kingdom, and the power, and the glory, forever. Amen.

TRUST AND COMFORT

Dear God,

I'm so glad You have made me aware to feel a mutual indifference between two people. Those are friendships that don't sustain us. Being deeply sensitive, very attentive and caring are so important to me. There are heartless mean people!! Some people never get what they want and some seem to constantly get everything they want like a magnet. I know that in the sweepstakes of a horse race, I got the golden ticket, a winner named "Bob!"

Are you someone who starts the day put together then slowly unravels during the course of the day? Some days you have to be the survivor of the fittest!

Have you been in a situation when you should have said something or done something when every single thing counted? Any regrets? We all hesitate because having the right to do it doesn't always mean it is right to do it.

Never underestimate the intelligence of someone. The truth will always come out. Don't put duty over love in any endeavor. Have a philosophy about your beliefs. Stand up for them. Don't violate your principles. Is your world black and white made up with simplicity more than difficulty?

We all have hobbies or talents that can empty our minds and quiet our thoughts. An infectious smile that brightens any room or personality and charm within a person are traits that are valuable achievements in life. Be there when someone needs help through a tough time. Remember joy can follow sadness by a simple act of touch. It says so much. Some people's faces show expressions like a window of their feelings. Love is a wonderful thing. Show it. Give it.

Our Father, who art in heaven, hallowed be Thy name. Thy kingdom come. Thy will be done on earth, as it is in heaven. Give us this day our daily bread. And forgive us our debts, as we forgive our debtors. And lead us not into temptation, but deliver us from evil. For Thine is the kingdom, and the power, and the glory, forever. Amen.

TRUST AND COMFORT

Dear God,

So many have lost a loved one recently. It's very difficult at times to face grief with a smile. And yet we know that You, God, will be with us. You always listen and hear and give us the strength to keep on going.

There is a peace that comes with the gift of memories that brings joy, quietness of love within my heart. Someone's path crosses mine to show me God's love.

The sun always stirs my energy. The stars and the moon remind me of another day of beauty. It's good to be alive!

Your love gives me peace of mind, keeps me kind and loving, and ready to lend a hand. There's always a good friend and You, God, a timeless gift!

Let us remember those who are going through difficult times and having health issues. Heal and help them, especially our Carol as she deals with cancer.

Our Father, who art in heaven, hallowed be Thy name. Thy kingdom come. Thy will be done on earth, as it is in heaven. Give us this day our daily bread. And forgive us our debts, as we forgive our debtors. And lead us not into temptation, but deliver us from evil. For Thine is the kingdom, and the power, and the glory, forever. Amen.

TRUST AND COMFORT

Dear God,

Sometimes there are no clear cut answers in life. We try to solve our problems with thought and care, patience and truth. We listen to our hearts versus what comes out of our mouths. Often the people you love most are given the least margin of error. Have a sympathetic ear. Are you aware how your personal experiences affect you? It can be good, or leave you with misgivings. Be perceptive in your choices, especially in critical times.

We may long for adventure, but we cherish the familiar. Have you ever felt like you were walking on air because your heart was so happy? Sometimes reentering the past is dangerous, or it can be good. Like rereading old letters, having a favorite blanket, remembering relatives we didn't care for.

Bringing up children who know they were a priority in your life satisfies a need in life. That need is two-fold: theirs and yours. Admire anyone who gently loves and forgives trespasses with understanding.

Do you talk at the graveside to your loved one? It creates a tender feeling towards everything and a rich appreciation for unfinished business.

Take a moment to pray. God is listening. I know God always answers, sometimes right away and sometimes the answer takes months. So hang in there. Trust Him. You will find new strength and peace of mind. I promise you.

Our Father, who art in heaven, hallowed be Thy name. Thy kingdom come. Thy will be done on earth, as it is in heaven. Give us this day our daily bread. And forgive us our debts, as we forgive our debtors. And lead us not into temptation, but deliver us from evil. For Thine is the kingdom, and the power, and the glory, forever. Amen.

TRUST AND COMFORT

Dear God,

Thank You for this opportunity to share my love for You and my personal feelings. What would I do without You in my life! I truly am so excited to live each day! It's so important to take care of our health. Our spirit will blossom in spite of bad days. Trust God. We make the choices that respond to our circumstances in our life that lead to our wellbeing and happiness.

Have flexibility and a listening heart. Have a sense of humor in your judgements because it puts a different perspective in your life. It helps conquer stress. Life is not only about what you get, but also about what is taken from us. Through loss we rediscover love and purpose. We all own a past even though we can't change it, and our past can be a strong motivator for our present life of happiness. It's wonderful to reflect and feel that you've done a good job with your circumstances. Thank You, God, for holding our lives together.

Have a smile to die for. Do you have a friend who touches your heart? That's a gift from God. Gut feelings are usually honest. Admit your wrongs. Hope is a powerful motivator. Know the person you spend time with and celebrate your joys and sorrows. Everything you say or do matters every day. Embrace it. Spiritual insight gives you wisdom about what beats in the heart of a person. Every day is a gift from God. There's nothing like the sight of a face that lights up when the person sees you. That's a heart moment!

Enjoy life at every chance because it can change like the wind. Worry more about the person that God wants you to be instead of your career. So live, understanding yourself with love. We need to really appreciate someone or something before it's too late.

Our Father, who art in heaven, hallowed be Thy name. Thy kingdom come. Thy will be done on earth as it is in heaven. Give us this day our daily bread. And forgive us our debts, as we forgive our debtors. And lead us not into temptation, but deliver us from evil. For Thine is the kingdom and the power, and the glory, forever. Amen.

TRUST AND COMFORT

Dear God,

We all have hopes and dreams and know that time is swift in passing. Set your tempo for your own life honestly. Remember friends and special moments of little things that can never be replaced. It's a journey spent with people you love. Teach us to bear the trials of life with You beside us for You alone know what is best for us by sending down the sunshine to make us feel renewed.

Do you know a couple that are like two peas in a pod? It's amazing how they act and think compared to a couple who are totally opposites in some things. Bob was always late and I was always an hour early. It's difficult to compromise! Some settle for the road less travelled and some never change.

So are you content with your life the way it is? Or do you need a new lease on life? Self-righteous people generally lack a sense of humor. We all make mistakes; the secret is being able to admit it. Some fathers find it difficult to speak verbally about their feelings for their children, but they show it in other ways. A loving relationship is the very breath of life. We have expectations and disappointments. Mixing it all up creates a different outcome for you.

Remember you own yourself with every facet of your own person. You are valuable. Have faith in yourself. Feeling an enveloping love from a person fills your being. Tell them how wonderful you think they are. It's wonderful to be loved and cared for instead of being alone at night. God has swept the worries and problems away and promises each one of us a new day. Trust Him.

Our Father, who art in heaven, hallowed be Thy name. Thy kingdom come. Thy will be done on earth, as it is in heaven. Give us this day our daily bread. And forgive us our debts, as we forgive our debtors. And lead us not into temptation, but deliver us from evil. For Thine is the kingdom, and the power, and the glory, forever. Amen.

TRUST AND COMFORT

Dear God,

Here I am again thanking You for another quiet moment. Have you ever had a day when it was difficult having kindness for yourself? Growing up did your parents ever give you advice about life and to this day you still remember it? My father always said you never have to be boastful about anything and be gentle and kind to everyone!! Have a sensitivity to the promise in life. Be a warm human being with inner strength to get you through life. Make it worthwhile with serenity and humor.

Do you think your life is the sum total of your experiences? If that's true, we should make a strong effort to make them the most memorable towards happiness. Cherish new experiences. So often we come alive when we accomplish something we thought we weren't capable of doing. One valuable lesson is to know who you are and what you have to give up to be that person.

Not everyone has someone to comfort them when times are tough. Love is the motivator for comfort!! Do you think love deepens responsibility? It's wonderful to be a part of a family and to celebrate holidays, hugs, smiles, tears, truths, respect, manners and harmony. You get attached to certain people and places. Within your home, is there a special room of your heart?

Life is about moving forward hopefully. Know that life will get better as you move hopefully through everything, especially with your children. Be like that one leaf that hangs on to a tree so tenaciously no matter what. Remember God's love, it's always there for you. Share your thoughts with Him. Make good life choices. It's hard to do some things you don't want to do or have regrets that you didn't try. We all make poor choices at times so celebrate the good choices because it's your blessing for life, and it's a forever thing.

Our Father, who art in heaven, hallowed be Thy name. Thy kingdom come. Thy will be done on earth, as it is in heaven. Give us this day our daily bread. And forgive us our debts, as we forgive our debtors. And lead us not into temptation, but deliver us from evil. For Thine is the kingdom, and the power, and the glory, forever. Amen.

TRUST AND COMFORT

Dear God,

All people grieve differently with the loss of a loved one, but how does one recover from the loss of a child? I know I had to forgive myself because I never got the chance to say good bye to my father and tell him how much I loved him. We can't change the past, only the future. Spend time with those you love best and feel God's constant love as you live day by day.

We drive ourselves with goals in life to succeed, and strive for more. Do we ever reach a point of contentment within our hearts? When a great challenge in your life occurs, and you know you have to fight it with integrity and the help of God, you will feel like a different person upon reflection. We need balance between work and play. We need quiet moments. Do you have a sixth sense for knowing the persona of a person or a situation? Feel close to some friends and family. Let them feel your wisdom, humor, and love because later might be too late.

As parents sometimes one of our children turns out to be a challenging ordeal—a test to the words "understanding" and "resentment" or having a "defensive attitude" about life. Remember that the tempo of life is filled with ups and downs. That's why special moments are so important. Love changes everything. Know who you are and like yourself.

In your travels have you ever been to a place that simply held you in awe with feelings of the beauty surrounding you? That's a "wow" moment. What the heart loves most is never lost. It gives new meaning to your life, so start each day with love in your heart.

Our Father, who art in heaven, hallowed be Thy name. Thy kingdom come. Thy will be done on earth, as it is in heaven. Give us this day our daily bread. And forgive us our debts, as we forgive our debtors. And lead us not into temptation, but deliver us from evil. For Thine is the kingdom, and the power, and the glory, forever. Amen.

TRUST AND COMFORT

Dear God,

A sunny day in winter reminds me of how You alone have touched my life so many times. I know how important it is to say, "I love you," have a smile, and give a hug to family and friends. They are the honesties in life, simple and true! Hold these close to your heart.

We have to learn to live each day through heartaches and pain. With God watching we will have hope to get through these times. So many times in life we have to weigh our options for the way to go with decisions. You'll know if you were right when your heart is happy. It's important to share your values and treat your loved ones with respect. Remember when the kids with their smiling faces believed in Santa and the tooth fairy? Have you ever had a day that went so well with happiness that you didn't want it to end?

Be optimistic in life. That alone will serve you well, and as it builds within you, you will feel a smile and feel happiness. Thank You, God. Have you ever met someone who looks like an angel and acts like one? It's not easy to be hopeful in all situations. However, remember what's important to you. Being kind to yourself boosts your own self esteem.

We all experience disappointments in life. This is when we learn whether we have resilience in dealing with it. Isn't it great to meet someone with a smile and an aura of gentleness? It renews our hope for a better world. We all do things differently. Be your own person by using your unique qualities. Try to be in a job that you love. You will never regret it. Many people depend on you. Take credit, when credit is due. You will feel happy. Reality can be cruel at times, but with God and time we can heal and move forward. It happens.

Our Father, who art in heaven, hallowed be Thy name. Thy kingdom come. Thy will be done on earth, as it is in heaven. Give us this day our daily bread. And forgive us our debts, as we forgive our debtors. And lead us not into temptation, but deliver us from evil. For Thine is the kingdom, and the power, and the glory, forever. Amen.

TRUST AND COMFORT

Dear God,

There's a field on Main Street not far from my house where a gorgeous scene unfolds. Fourteen deer gather at dusk before they head into the woods. The building of new homes has taken away a lot of the woods for animals.

When things are going your way you feel great, but how about when they don't? Do you handle it well? What about gut feelings? Are they generally right? When you go through heartaches, God will help you through the scars of life. Family and friends help by bearing each other's burden with thoughtfulness and love. Miracles do happen. I am so grateful for each day because of what I've endured. It has made me a better person.

Whatever you allow into your heart is your choice. We should strive to make life sweet and tranquil. To enjoy it, have some lazy moments. Listen to the rain beating down on your roof. Relax. Have trust and commitment in what you do. Feel joy. True happiness really radiates and is felt by all who are with you. Time spent with family and friends is a gift from God wrapped in a beautiful package. Enjoy it.

Do you smile when you remember something that nobody else knows? With time bad things that happened in your past become tolerable memories. In life we have to extend the olive branch and learn to say, "I'm sorry." It's not a good idea to be on the bad attitude list. Have you ever given advice to your children or a friend and felt it went in one ear and out the other? Is your family and loved one of your heart in everything you do? Remember moments make our lives.

Our Father, who art in heaven, hallowed be Thy name. Thy kingdom come. Thy will be done on earth, as it is in heaven. Give us this day our daily bread. And forgive us our debts, as we forgive our debtors. And lead us not into temptation, but deliver us from evil. For Thine is the kingdom, and the power, and the glory, forever. Amen.

TRUST AND COMFORT

Dear God,

When trouble hits our lives, and the load is heavy, we need to try and remember how many times God has reached out to us with love to get us back on the upward climb, time after time. So make room for God in your heart. He will always touch you with grace. Make time for a quiet "me" moment. You will live a better and happier life. Embrace a new outlook on life with new insight and discover that the key to life is love.

Enjoy simple bits within your day. Be in the moment. Radiate warmth in your personality. Take the time do what you want to do. Is there something special that defines you as a person? Recognize what you can give of value to others in any situation. Never sell yourself short. The bright side of life always produces opportunity. Family also means commitment to each other. It's a reflection of God's love, and so is a true friend.

Listen to your children, and smile with them. They have different reasons for what they do, and we want to try and understand them. That's a chapter in our lives as parents. It's a testimony of our love for them. I love it when I see closeness and cozy love within a family.

Is fall a time when you feel closer to God with your spiritual memories? What your heart has loved most will always be precious to you like some special people or family. Be generous. It's so uplifting to your being. There's a special peace that comes to you when you live in your home with happiness. Feel loved. Feel new meaning in little things that brighten your day. With love comes quiet serenity. Thank You, God for every day, and thank You for Your love.

Our Father, who art in heaven, hallowed be Thy name. Thy kingdom come. Thy will be done on earth, as it is in heaven. Give us this day our daily bread. And forgive us our debts, as we forgive our debtors. And lead us not into temptation, but deliver us from evil. For Thine is the kingdom, and the power, and the glory, forever. Amen.

TRUST AND COMFORT

Dear God,

When you lose someone you love, their spirit remains with you for you to carry on, reminding you to continue living a life with happiness with the help of God. Look inwardly at yourself and realize that life is so worthwhile. We can gain wisdom with change. Don't waste it away. Follow your heart. God wants us to experience joy. Small, thoughtful gestures can really sweeten a relationship. Bob was a master at that!

Strive to be compassionate and generous toward family, friends, and people. Think of what you would do if you were in their shoes. We all have habits we do every day on "cruise control." I know I do. Think about it. Some habits we acquired when we were young, and some we acquired as we aged. I find now when shopping, I only purchase what really sings to me. Notice the scenery around you because real happiness involves searching, striving for, and growing to achieve that.

Have you ever felt you earned your place in life? God gave you this life, so take care of it. When heartache hits, your life and family and friends, say, "I love you," and "We're here for you." That's God's grace touching your spirit. It's a reason to live. Life is too precious and short beyond measure.

Feel the hand of God. Love and respect yourself. Have music in your life. It fills you with happiness and dance. Sometimes the hardest choices in life aren't between right and wrong; instead it's what's right and best! People define you by what you say and do, so when you lose everything in one part of your life you are left with a valuable memory. New thoughts can change your life. Know the person you want to be.

Our Father, who art in heaven, hallowed be Thy name. Thy kingdom come. Thy will be done on earth, as it is in heaven. Give us this day our daily bread. And forgive us our debts, as we forgive our debtors. And lead us not into temptation, but deliver us from evil. For Thine is the kingdom, and the power, and the glory, forever. Amen.

TRUST AND COMFORT

Dear God,

When problems hit me, one of my favorite prayers is "Let not your heart be troubled, ye believe in God, believe also in me." (John 14:1) It has worked for me as a calming balm forever.

This is October and breast cancer month. In this room some of you are great cancer survivors. Some of you may not know that I am a breast cancer survivor. I didn't have clean margins, so I had major surgery and treatment. It's been 16 years since that day. I can't imagine surviving without the people here at church and the Visiting Nurses who came every day. I received food and visits from this church family. We prayed together for my healing, and I felt love. God blessed me. I'm doing great. After all that at 86, I am on no medications. In the morning four vitamins, oatmeal, 30 minutes of exercise, and prayer keep me healthy and moving. I have reasons to be ferociously thankful and cheerful! Miracles do happen.

Be content in your life and enjoy it with humor. Have a partnership of trust in yourself and others. It deepens friendship and love. Do you ever think about when you'll have a chance to enjoy life? Sometimes we have to cut back on things to accomplish that. It's worth it in our journey of life. Be sure of your choice in a career and love it because if you love what you're doing, you will excel at it! We all need more heart and more spirit and gratitude to God.

If you can avoid tension and controversy, most things end up fine. It's your life so enjoy every minute. Bad neighbors can make your life miserable, so try to be neutral just like Switzerland. Don't do something when your heart isn't in it. Isn't it odd how we give "control" people so much power over us? Vital moments in life need you to stand up for yourself. We all need balance, stability, happiness, and energy. We only have one life to live, so believe in yourself and God.

Our Father, who art in heaven, hallowed be Thy name. Thy kingdom come. Thy will be done on earth, as it is in heaven. Give us this day our daily bread. And forgive us our debts, as we forgive our debtors. And lead us not into temptation, but deliver us from evil. For Thine is the kingdom, and the power, and the glory, forever. Amen.

TRUST AND COMFORT

Dear God,

Thank You for the moon in the sky and the sprinkle of stars at night. It's a beautiful gift. Have you ever had a night with sleepless sleep? On reflection of your life do you feel that it has changed for the better? Even though we all go through difficult times it also brings us to a healing, quality time. Nature empathizes with us and complements our mood. Our family and friends are a gift from God with values of love and trust for day-to-day living.

So often we wait for a death in a family to do better to those who are living. As we age, we must continue to exercise and walk. It's an investment to your health and life. Open up your heart so you can feel deeper. Take deep breaths. It's not easy when your life has always contained the word "we" to go to the word "I." So look inwardly to yourself one moment at a time. God is there for you. Feel His warmth within your own rhythm for life.

Do you know someone who absolutely brings a smile to your face? That's inner joy. It's better to have loved and lost than not loved at all. Aging with a deeper sense of appreciation for so many things including love, health, friends, family, and home is fantastic. You are the captain of your soul. I truly am so happy to wake up to another day. Thank You, God.

A true friend that is yours cannot be replaced. Each is a reflection of God's love. Do you have some special memories from your past that even today still inspire and touch your heart? We can't ever go back to what we were. That's life in all honesty; however, we can move forward with winning or losing, success or failure because the result is what makes us the person we've become through the process.

Our Father, who art in heaven, hallowed be Thy name. Thy kingdom come. Thy will be done on earth, as it is in heaven. Give us this day our daily bread. And forgive us our debts, as we forgive our debtors. And lead us not into temptation, but deliver us from evil. For Thine is the kingdom, and the power, and the glory, forever. Amen.

BEING THANKFUL

Dear God,

When attention and technique and talent come together it creates a miracle. God gave us Karen, and we are truly blessed! With Karen our own hearts are touched along with the people who hear us when we sing to the glory of God. That is a magic moment!

Do you have a favorite day of the week? I only dislike Monday for some reason. Seems most people dress for church in their better clothes, not in their grubbies.

Gardens change with each season, except for winter, when it rests to replenish itself for months to come. That is an example for our lives! We need to thank God for a good life, our family and show a kind heart. Calmness, humbleness and gratitude are some of the keys to a satisfying life. Live and learn!! You are His creation. Hold His hand.

When you feel like there aren't enough hours in a day, and you start to feel stressed, you should STOP!! Take a deep breath. Close your eyes and bring up a thought of a beautiful place or person. It works wonders! Are you a person who can fall asleep at a moment's notice? Bob always could. My daughter Susie starts relaxing, and closes her eyes whenever I'm talking to her. It's almost comical.

Try to keep a balance in any situation even when dealing with horrible people!! Always tell your husband or someone you love that the best present you ever received in life was them!! Make life meaningful and you will be happy.

Our Father, who art in heaven, hallowed be Thy name. Thy kingdom come. Thy will be done on earth, as it is in heaven. Give us this day our daily bread. And forgive us our debts, as we forgive our debtors. And lead us not into temptation, but deliver us from evil. For Thine is the kingdom, and the power, and the glory, forever. Amen.

BEING THANKFUL

Dear God,

I like to start my day with You. Thank You for another day! That's so awesome! You know how much I enjoy each day! You have always put well-meaning friends in my path with encouragement, or their prevention in doing things the wrong way. We are all vulnerable. Have you noticed that decisions made amongst good friends are usually instinctive with all five senses operating?

Truthfully there are far more good days in your life than bad! Love should always be shared, not hidden, or simply stored within. It's part of your happy life! As parents, we have to have belief in ourselves first, the pay-off is huge. There is no accounting for happiness the way it turns up surprisingly in your life. It gives us comfort within to know that it's God's grace. Share your happiness. In China the color yellow symbolizes happiness. A house is just a house, but with love within, it becomes a home! Acts of love speak louder than words.

Do you think that everything happens for a reason? Live day by day, moment to moment in what you do. Be astute about mistakes so that you only have to learn that lesson once. It's sad if you realize that the most important things in your life passed by and it may be too late to do anything about it. Sometimes we get a second chance to right it—especially if it's someone we love. Have you ever thought about how one phone call can change your life? It can be good or bad news!!

Our Father, who art in heaven, hallowed be Thy name. Thy kingdom come. Thy will be done on earth, as it is in heaven. Give us this day our daily bread. And forgive us our debts, as we

forgive our debtors. And lead us not into temptation, but deliver us from evil. For Thine is the kingdom, and the power, and the glory, forever. Amen.

BEING THANKFUL

Dear God,

This morning is filled with beautiful sunshine. Thank You, God. I love it! Never let age define your feelings. Personally, I live beyond feelings. I'm usually happy with a knowledge of my limitations. Be honest with yourself. We all make mistakes. Admitting them and dealing with them is our salvation to happiness. I have learned that what you say and do has far reaching results. Have you ever had someone or something that impacted your life to make it better? I know for sure that God has touched me. I know singing in this choir with Karen and being with all of you has made me feel touched in all dimensions to make my life happier with joy and love.

We all have the opportunity to travel and deepen our spiritual journey with God. Take time out to remember to look at the stars that God has placed for you. It's a beautiful moment. Some happy moments are felt when you jump out and do something different. Learn not to be so rigid and predictable. We all should have a special niche—a home where we can relax and enjoy that feeling of peace and comfort. It's a privilege to be alive. Enjoy that moment. Just wearing color will put you in a good mood. Try it—you'll like it! And being kind to others and yourself is so easy. You'll feel good having a tender heart.

Do you know someone who is all "hard shell" on the outside, but is soft as a marshmallow inwardly? As partners, closeness and chemistry are important with love, so is thoughtfulness, respect and kindness. Inner peace is that joy that God gives to you as a gift. It can work miracles inside of you. Believe me, it happens. The rush of day to day living makes us want quiet peace within ourselves. A smile of a loved one can do that. Share your love of life. It changes everything.

Our Father, who art in heaven, hallowed be Thy name. Thy kingdom come. Thy will be done on earth as it is in heaven. Give us this day our daily bread. And forgive us our debts, as we forgive our debtors. And lead us not into temptation, but deliver us from evil. For Thine is the kingdom and the power, and the glory, forever. Amen.

BEING THANKFUL

Dear God,

Thank You for my 85th birthday! You know me so well. You know how I truly enjoy every day. It's funny the way things work out in life. Have you ever thought about being close to the person you love who always made you feel safe and happy? Look into their eyes and feel their love and strength, calmness and humor. Life is a lesson. Personalities are opposites in some areas.

Bob was always late. I was always an hour early. Is being who you are the result of how you were raised more than blood lines? Mellowness comes with a good marriage. The past is the past. Work on the present.

I like to live life abundantly. I enjoy this place, this moment. Relationships with people, special occasions and circumstances give me vitality. Be gentle with people. Over time be a true friend! Self-importance is secondary to a cheery disposition. Being a team player isn't easy for everyone. You have that option. Life goes on but it also stalls at times just like a car does.

Is it important where you live? More than how you live? Make sure of your footing in this world. Have a friendly chat and read a book. We all need friends. We need someone to spur us on to learn new things and try some. We shouldn't just exist; that's a hollow life! Lean on God. He will give you the strength to act. Your family is His gift to you. His presence is the calming balm we all need. It's that quiet peace. Enjoy this passage of time, that's another gift from God.

Our Father, who art in heaven, hallowed be Thy name. Thy kingdom come. Thy will be done on earth, as it is in heaven. Give us this day our daily bread. And forgive us our debts, as we forgive our debtors. And lead us not into temptation, but deliver us from evil. For Thine is the kingdom, and the power, and the glory, forever. Amen.

BEING THANKFUL

Dear God,

Thank You for our beautiful concert and for Karen who plans and leads this choir. She is blessed with so much talent, and we are blessed to interpret music that leaves us with a sweet contentment.

Isn't it wonderful to wake up and start a whole new day? Most of them are happy ones with a few touched by tears. Remember God can look into your heart. One of the good things about getting older is we learn what is important in our lives including paths we take and the people we love who make a wonderful difference.

Sometimes people are defined by their good works, or their bad. Do something you really love to do. Feel the joy of giving. Bring back a memory that will put a smile on your face like Bob loving strawberry jam and a bowl of ice cream before bedtime.

Be kind to yourself. Chances are you'll enjoy the life you're living. Know your God. He can lift your heavy heart. Enjoy the sun's warmth, the salty smell of the ocean or a walk on the beach. Give a hug to your child. Be a good listener for your older married children; they need hugs, too. Emotions of the heart are a beautiful, encompassing thing. They are our truest wealth of the earth.

Our Father, who art in heaven, hallowed be Thy name. Thy kingdom come. Thy will be done on earth, as it is in heaven. Give us this day our daily bread. And forgive us our debts, as we forgive our debtors. And lead us not into temptation, but deliver us from evil. For Thine is the kingdom, and the power, and the glory, forever. Amen.

BEING THANKFUL

Dear God,

I never heard of Thanksgiving before I came to America. What a beautiful holiday when families and friends get together with love. I embrace the day. I asked my daughter if I could gather the family to read them my prayer I'd written. I didn't know how the 14 to 24 year olds would accept it. It was wonderful. They hugged me and told me I blew them away!

At some point in our life, we gather experience, wisdom and perspective. Sometimes we attempt something outside our comfort zone. That prayer time surprised me—God was there—some things that happen in life have no answer. You, who are teachers, know and feel that there are some children who you'll not be able to teach; you can't reach them, but you still keep trying.

Miracles. One happened here in this church when John gave one of his kidneys to Phyllis. That was a "higher Being" moment!! Saving a person's life!! Think about how you may have a child who either looks a lot like you, or has some of your mannerisms. Appreciate the time spent with your children or grandchildren when they arrange their stuffed animals on their beds for sleep.

Enjoy the sun's warmth or helping someone in a wheel chair get into the pool with a noodle or a memory of Bob listening to classical music in his truck. We were married 64 years ago today.

So, have an operative word for a day, like "kindness" or "laughter." You will feel so much happier.

Our Father, who art in heaven, hallowed be Thy name. Thy kingdom come. Thy will be done on earth, as it is in heaven. Give us this day our daily bread. And forgive us our debts, as we forgive our debtors. And lead us not into temptation, but deliver us from evil. For Thine is the kingdom, and the power, and the glory, forever. Amen.

BEING THANKFUL

Dear God,

Today when I went to Stop & Shop I was greeted by a lady who said, "Thank you for all the notes you've written to me. You have no idea how much it helped." Her son had just graduated, so his best friend was in the car with him. An accident occurred and the son killed his best friend. He is now in the Plymouth jail. We all bear some crosses at some time in our lives, but comfort comes with it also. That is a moment, a blessing of love from God.

When you feel your inner soul, have you ever felt God on the journey with you? Be thankful for your life. That is like music to God. See, hear, and feel each day. God cares for you. Life's clock is like a thief, ticking away. Don't lie to yourself. Be the individual you can be. One never knows the outcome of a deed done. The gift of life every day is precious with no price tag. It's yours to enjoy with all your heart, or to let it pass by in a "comme ci, comme ça" way.

All things work together from tears to laughter. God provides the inner vision through prayer. Recall a special moment. A loved one's kiss, quiet peaceful hours. Treat others with kindness each day. Surely a heart that's happy is a heart that is free.

Our Father, who art in heaven, hallowed be Thy name. Thy kingdom come. Thy will be done on earth, as it is in heaven. Give us this day our daily bread. And forgive us our debts, as we forgive our debtors. And lead us not into temptation, but deliver us from evil. For Thine is the kingdom, and the power, and the glory, forever. Amen.

BEING THANKFUL

Dear God,

Old age doesn't always mean being set in our ways! We're aware that we must enjoy the years left to us. Like Althea jumping out of a plane in her 70s! She's awesome!! Enjoy each day even if you're not in retirement. I'm enjoying the simplicity of my life the way it is each day.

Technology is great, but it has also taken away the personal touch of conversation with people. Remember listening to just a radio? Today our grandchildren are texting 24/7 and sending snap "camera shots" within one gadget! We always want the best for our children. Life is made up of change, there is no escaping it.

Moments of warmth within a family, memories happy and sad, help you discover your own worth and to move forward to a new pace of life and future. Small acts of helping others, laughter and love, make our own life better. Notice things that are happening when you go for a walk!! It's a good thing.

English boarding school taught me discipline, neatness, sharing, friendship and harmony. Those friendships established continued after I came to America. I never expected to attend a "China Hands" reunion 20 years later and to see so many people I grew up with in Shanghai. There were 1,500 of us who survived. That was a "wow" moment. Good relationships depend on love and respect as a bonding ingredient.

In life, you have a bad day, and the very next day you could feel love and joy and a chance of another day. I've noticed as we age, we check on our friends and neighbors more often, especially if they live alone. So give gifts of love and you will be happy.

Our Father, who art in heaven, hallowed be Thy name. Thy kingdom come. Thy will be done on earth, as it is in heaven. Give us this day our daily bread. And forgive us our debts, as we forgive our debtors. And lead us not into temptation, but deliver us from evil. For Thine is the kingdom, and the power, and the glory, forever. Amen.

BEING THANKFUL

Dear God,

Here I am again enjoying spring, the choir of birds in the yard, squirrels, forsythia, and rises of tulips and daffodils. There is so much joy in some things, like feeding the birds.

Have you ever been overwhelmed not knowing if you were coming or going? Trying so hard to figure a piece of the puzzle in life that just won't fit? We all need to take time to reflect and relax. You will feel like a new person.

We are so lucky to be in this choir, as we are God's guardian angels. Feel the love. We are never prepared for failures—we keep on trying—your heart will tell you when you're right.

We meet a lot of people in our lives, but only some make it into our hearts. During a problem time with one of your children don't you hate asking questions for the truth fearing the answers you might get? That's a scary moment!

There are days we will remember forever. Bad habits die hard, and good ones take time to flourish. Hang in there! All of us need someone who loves us, and who will forgive us for a wrong doing. Good intentions are just good intentions if not carried out with an effort. For one I don't leave dirty dishes in the sink to greet me "Good Morning!"

Each day, with my simple short prayers, I feel God's love. Thank You, God. Today, can you think of something you're truly grateful for? It's so great to see and feel a family that has that "magic togetherness" of affection. Many people never experience it. Fear is difficult to deal with. I know I lived with it under the Japanese for years, losing our home and feeling constant hunger. What would I have done without prayer? I prayed a lot and God blessed me!

I'm here in America. I love this place and the people, starting with our leader in choir, Karen. God is always listening to you. His love gives you the strength to tackle anything. God feels everything we go through, good and bad. We become a better person. I do dance around my kitchen every day and sing like a nut case. That's how I truly feel. I'm so happy to be alive to enjoy my family and friends. So make room in your heart for God.

Our Father, who art in heaven, hallowed be Thy name. Thy kingdom come. Thy will be done on earth, as it is in heaven. Give us this day our daily bread. And forgive us our debts, as we forgive our debtors. And lead us not into temptation, but deliver us from evil. For Thine is the kingdom, and the power, and the glory, forever. Amen.

BEING THANKFUL

Dear God,

Spring is so wonderful to lift your face to the sun again, and to see daffodils bloom and the showy magnolias and forsythia—it's beautiful! Do you have a favorite time of year?

There are days as parents we get tired of delivering lectures about the same issue. Some children have a religious objection to keeping their room neat, rinsing out their dishes, helping with laundry, not to mention vacuuming and Windexing! It's hysterical! They think the good fairy or Cinderella comes to do it all! As a mother, how do you define yourself? Are you loving, protective, accepting, and caring? Having children is one thing. Raising them is another. It takes strength and courage to stand up for what you think is right.

What would life be without stress and responsibilities? We also need an aura of kindness and patience to establish a grounded sense of right and wrong to make life worthwhile. You can understand some things, but it doesn't mean you have to like it! We are all victims of what life deals out. Each of us handles it in a different way. Our inner thoughts and feelings belong to each of us personally, unless we choose to share it.

Do you have a fear of something? Mine is lightening. When you do anything in life, really do it with everything you have. Live life as it comes. It's not easy, but necessary! Sharing is good for the soul and love softens something in you and it never goes away. Put your heart in your hand. Time goes by fast. Without a yesterday you can't concentrate on today. So thank God for His timeless grace and love day after day.

Our Father, who art in heaven, hallowed be Thy name. Thy kingdom come. Thy will be done on earth, as it is in heaven. Give us this day our daily bread. And forgive us our debts, as we forgive our debtors. And lead us not into temptation, but deliver us from evil. For Thine is the kingdom, and the power, and the glory, forever. Amen.

BEING THANKFUL

Dear God,

Here we are again at the time of three crosses that stood upon a troubled hill, feeling that solemn hour, that sacred spot of glory. You remind us that even through kindness and death, Your love and spirit continue to live in the bright daffodils, forsythia, crocus, and robins.

We have so much to be joyful about. I can truly say that even though my Bob is gone, his spirit and Yours is always with me. I feel it and that is an unbelievable gift to me. Every day something happens to each one of us and the secret is to take the time to savor that moment. It might be just a "small" thing.

For me, getting off a busy highway and getting home makes me so happy. I'm always thanking You, God, aren't I? I'm happy just being alive and healthy to enjoy each day and all that it encompasses—our family, home, friends, a cup of coffee, hot water, food, church, freedom. This country is a wonderful place—it is full with the goodness of God. Look around you, then smile and thank God for yourself.

Our Father, who art in heaven, hallowed be Thy name. Thy kingdom come. Thy will be done on earth, as it is in heaven. Give us this day our daily bread. And forgive us our debts, as we forgive our debtors. And lead us not into temptation, but deliver us from evil. For Thine is the kingdom, and the power, and the glory, forever. Amen.

BEING THANKFUL

Dear God,

It's so comforting to me to be in the home where Bob grew up. I also had three out of my four children there! There are lots of memories and improvements. I was always certain of my welcome and familiarity—it's a great feeling!

On reflection of my life, I have found out that we can develop new strength and faith, new peace of mind, and new deeper gratefulness for everything. In your persona, are you cautious and think things through? Or do you take risks and chance it? When someone physically hurts you, you never forget it, but you can work towards feeling that it doesn't matter and continue living. Sadly it does eliminate the feeling of love towards that person. Commitment by itself is one thing, but "love and commitment" is a whole new equation.

Look into your heart and know what's in it. You see I was badly beaten constantly by my mother. My sister will tell you that English boarding school was my salvation!! I'm sure my joie de vivre for life is one result of it. We need to nourish our souls with happiness. We can control only so much of our lives, the rest is up to God.

Be with people who love you—have spirit and warmth and responsibility. You will evolve as a person with positive characteristics of healing and understanding. Do you put everything you do with your whole heart and soul? Successful careers don't always guarantee successful personal lives. Take pleasure doing things with people you enjoy. Do you have a special place that takes away your tension and restores you? Ogunquit is mine.

Aren't you amazed at the end of the day for what you have accomplished? That's God's blessing. Why is it we always regret what we don't do, rather than what we do? There are days when you can feel all your senses operating together to give you joy. Are you a warm cuddly person? A lot of people aren't. Do you think our children are an extension of ourselves? Thank God for the gift of family and friends, for persons who changed your heart and life forever. Feel that wholeness. Thank God.

Our Father, who art in heaven, hallowed be Thy name. Thy kingdom come. Thy will be done on earth, as it is in heaven. Give us this day our daily bread. And forgive us our debts, as we forgive our debtors. And lead us not into temptation, but deliver us from evil. For Thine is the kingdom, and the power, and the glory, forever. Amen.

BEING THANKFUL

Dear God,

I have learned that even through heartaches, I can find contentment in celebrating my handicapped son's 64th birthday today. Children's Hospital didn't think he would live to be 40!! I am so thankful for all these extra years. Thank You for all Your love and care within this life of mine.

Our Father, who art in heaven, hallowed be Thy name. Thy kingdom come. Thy will be done on earth, as it is in heaven. Give us this day our daily bread. And forgive us our debts, as we forgive our debtors. And lead us not into temptation, but deliver us from evil. For Thine is the kingdom, and the power, and the glory, forever. Amen.

BEING THANKFUL

Dear God,

Holy Week is so emotional. Sadness, joy, and triumphant music fill our souls! It's a true reminder that life may be as it is, or life can be as you make it. In hopeless moments, suffering hurts. The inner emotions of our minds and hearts can triumph and bring laughter and be a beautiful thing. Happiness can come out of horror. Young people have their whole lives before them. Add dimension to your life. Be good neighbors. Love your family.

When I think of Bob, I feel kindness, love and thoughtfulness. He took the time to turn my car around so that I faced out towards Main Street!! He knew I was the world's worst backer-upper that failed every day. After I made it to my lamp post, I always thanked God for my success, and I'd laugh at myself about it!!

He truly took the best care of me. He taught me so many things that helped me to live like a dragon not accepting defeat and to try leaping into situations with strength like a tiger. Thank You, God, for 58 years with Bob and thank You, God, for being in my life.

Our Father, who art in heaven, hallowed be Thy name. Thy kingdom come. Thy will be done on earth, as it is in heaven. Give us this day our daily bread. And forgive us our debts, as we forgive our debtors. And lead us not into temptation, but deliver us from evil. For Thine is the kingdom, and the power, and the glory, forever. Amen.

BEING THANKFUL

Dear God,

With You in my life, I never feel alone and within this fabric of existence, in spite of grim and horrendous happenings, You restore my soul. You continue to bless me with a sense of home and gratitude, love and kindness, day after day. I believe in You, and that a family houses souls, along with love and treasured friends.

I've learned that without compassion we should make no judgments. We need unconditional love for ourselves and others. Happiness is the "uncle" you never knew about. It comes to a child whose mother has passed out from alcohol, to a dog chewing on a bone, to a clerk stacking cans of carrots at night in a market, and to you when you hear rain falling on the open sea, or on the roof of your home. Thank You, God.

Where would we be in life without faith? Have you ever met someone who is critical and unhappy? The word "never" is an extraordinary word, when you apply it to yourself! We all have to face responsibilities and some can be unpleasant. Being secretive with a bad attitude is not a good legacy for anyone!

Have you ever thought or said "good riddance" about a person or incident? I have. Every parent needs a break sometime. You have to do what's right for you in spite of pressures to do it differently. It's difficult not to get involved in your children's relationships when they come complaining to you, especially if your vibes are sending you signals. Be careful what you say privately or publicly, it's a sensitive nature problem.

Time measured in minutes should be enjoyed with joy and happiness. It can change at a snap of a finger. Have new strength, new peace of mind, and reflect on your contentment—facial expressions tell a story of your feelings—make it a joyful one.

Our Father, who art in heaven, hallowed be Thy name. Thy kingdom come. Thy will be done on earth, as it is in heaven. Give us this day our daily bread. And forgive us our debts, as we forgive our debtors. And lead us not into temptation, but deliver us from evil. For Thine is the kingdom, and the power, and the glory, forever. Amen.

BEING THANKFUL

Dear God,

I love starting each day in prayer—it is quiet and peaceful with my thoughts of You. I feel thankful for all the special things You do. Some of you know I have a handicapped son, Dickie. He was born in the Army hospital in Shanghai. The next day the colonel came to tell us that Dickie couldn't breathe because of an enlarged thymus gland and that he had made arrangements at a French hospital for radiation treatments. It took three treatments to shrink the thymus. We then had to leave for America because the Communists were gaining in power. All Americans were told to leave.

Our son seemed fine. By one-and-a-half to two-years-old he couldn't walk or talk. Special boots were made for him with metal inserts. He never cried, mostly happy and eating. Children's Hospital was great. The test results were heartbreaking. I had never seen Bob cry!! Evidently my body living with hunger for so many years under the Japanese was the main culprit in Dickie's developmental process. For a while my pregnancy halted, but instead of miscarrying, it started up again.

Today, at 64, he still can't read or write. He's in a knee brace and he lives happily with four other severely handicapped in Carver with such good care. Judi and I go and take him out for lunch on a weekend. Hardships can tear people apart or make them closer. For us, we had no regrets. We kept him home with us as long as we could. Seeing him happy is the reward for us. Do I blame myself? No. I was nineteen and in love.

God, thank You for three other healthy children. I love You.

Our Father, who art in heaven, hallowed be Thy name. Thy kingdom come. Thy will be done on earth, as it is in heaven. Give us this day our daily bread. And forgive us our debts, as we forgive our debtors. And lead us not into temptation, but deliver us from evil. For Thine is the kingdom, and the power, and the glory, forever. Amen.

FAMILY AND FRIENDS

Dear God,

Have you ever had a friend who was like a second mother? She was funny, sharp, and a listener for all your problems? That is a special bond. There is no escape built over time from memories, so hold some of them close to you. Every day your present becomes your past in your lifetime. The passage of time is a funny thing. Sometimes you want to stop time and hold on for just a moment, especially if it's a "Hallmark" moment.

Reality has a way of interrupting even when you think you can sleep your troubles away. Have you ever thought that there is a God's way and plan as life goes on? It's a gift. We never know what's ahead, even though we never stop planning. We survive, we move on through sadness and joy, humor and inner calm.

Sometimes a touch is better than talk. Marriage means compromise for both parties. The world doesn't revolve around one person. You who are teachers know how a pupil makes you smile and feel when they turn out well, fulfilling their destiny. Parents are also blessed when their children do likewise.

Didn't you love going to things your children or grandchildren did? Chorus, sports, school plays? We as adults can act as children when we think no one is looking. Our children need to go out into the world and follow their hearts, making their own mistakes, experiencing pain and hurt and rejection, but also love, laughter and joy.

Life is a lesson. If you are loved and believe in God, you are never alone.

Our Father, who art in heaven, hallowed be Thy name. Thy kingdom come. Thy will be done on earth, as it is in heaven. Give us this day our daily bread. And forgive us our debts, as we forgive our debtors. And lead us not into temptation, but deliver us from evil. For Thine is the kingdom, and the power, and the glory, forever. Amen.

FAMILY AND FRIENDS

Dear God,

Being a transplant from Shanghai, China, I love being where I am. Everyone is capable of change! It's funny about the stages in life—insecurities as teens turn into insecurities of middle age, then old age, with its host of issues. You have to know what motivates you. When you lose someone you love, you begin a journey of self-discovery. Love and respect have to be freely given. Respect is something earned, love comes with no limits attached. However, you have to like yourself enough to have a good relationship. Small gestures of love are always welcome, as we go through life's problems to come out on top.

Life is so much easier shared with someone. As we age, our needs change. For some it's a once in a lifetime love, and some never find it. So be a good partner to the one you love. Children within the same family are so different, one can be so needy and one so independent. Remember they will grow up and leave you to move on. So focus on your own life in balance, we need happiness and friendships, too.

Are you an ordinary person living in a world that loves extraordinary people? Bob was an advocate and champion helping me realize my hopes and dreams. He had faith in me! You have a choice of what you allow to enter into your heart. How your life is or can be is your choice.

Do some parents wreck the first part of a child's life? I'm so afraid it happens more often than not. Have you teared up from a memory out of the blue even though your life has been going well? It happens. Give yourself a hug and then smile. You'll be good to go.

Our Father, who art in heaven, hallowed be Thy name. Thy kingdom come. Thy will be done on earth, as it is in heaven. Give us this day our daily bread. And forgive us our debts, as we forgive our debtors. And lead us not into temptation, but deliver us from evil. For Thine is the kingdom, and the power, and the glory, forever. Amen.

FAMILY AND FRIENDS

Dear God,

Today I honor my brother Mario, the baby of the family. He died at 78, May 3, 2013. I was close to him and my other brother Sonny, especially surviving World War II in Shanghai, China. Growing up, he was always the good looking one. Always popular!

He really established his career in America and did well. His voice was like velvet. People loved hearing him, be it on TV, radio or hosting. He was intelligent and athletic and had charisma with people. I'm sure Bob was there to welcome him. So when major trauma hits, try to be with family or friends and some normal routine. It's important to remember the little things in life, just as much as the big ones.

I'm sure one of his happy thoughts like mine was coming to America. Not just as a refuge of peace, but a feeling of coming home!! Honesties in life give you happiness, a quiet faith that sustains you. Know that God alone has the answers.

Not all of us attain the goals we set. However, we can still be content with less. Believe in yourself by doing the best that you can, even though we miss the mark we set. Count your blessings. The easy way out isn't always the best solution.

Many people are good with their hands. Some have creative minds, some have discipline and ambition. To do well in something, you have to like it. Life is full of maybes, but some things are worth a risk. Instinct and timing is essential. Learn to live with many things. Life's too short for hassles!

Two people can make a great team. Be heartfelt in your endeavor and you will feel loved. Take God's hand in yours, and you will know how to enjoy every day.

Our Father, who art in heaven, hallowed be Thy name. Thy kingdom come. Thy will be done on earth, as it is in heaven. Give us this day our daily bread. And forgive us our debts, as we forgive our debtors. And lead us not into temptation, but deliver us from evil. For Thine is the kingdom, and the power, and the glory, forever. Amen.

FAMILY AND FRIENDS

Dear God,

I think if we're honest with ourselves we can admit to having too much on our plate, too much on our mind, and too much in our hearts. We might have said things and done things we regretted. We need to mend the bridges of communication before they get irreplaceable. Love has a healing power for uncomfortable truths. Quarrels and fights in a family can be resolved if we learn from them. Generally there's one person who brings everyone together. Feel peace and love take over your body. Be amongst people who care for you. Love your children wherever they are. We get brutally sentimental when our children become wonderful, caring adults. Your heart gets filled and you feel like crying.

Cross one bridge at a time. Never jeopardize a friendship. Be loyal to the people you love. Some people not only want to control the environment, but also people. Be discreet and efficient, but being personal puts a different dynamic on a situation.

If you are married to someone who is on the road weeks at a time, remember that they need undeniable love. They also need values which connect people. Humor helps cut tension. Have faith in God. There's a fine line between horrible and hilarious!

Do you remember a special place in your home like the kitchen table where homework was done, meals eaten, and important decisions were discussed and made? That made your day. Surprisingly, you often find out that what you lack, your family owns in talent, and that makes loving easier.

It's so important to be with someone who understands your rhythm and who wants what we can give to each other day to day. Isn't the first cup of coffee in the morning the best? Enjoy the ride and be happy.

Our Father, who art in heaven, hallowed be Thy name. Thy kingdom come. Thy will be done on earth, as it is in heaven. Give us this day our daily bread. And forgive us our debts, as we forgive our debtors. And lead us not into temptation, but deliver us from evil. For Thine is the kingdom, and the power, and the glory, forever. Amen.

FAMILY AND FRIENDS

Dear God,

What a beautiful fall morning! Makes us think about time spent with family and loved ones—a friendly chat, a time to read—some fun thing enjoyed for the evening. Life is our journey with You, God, a place where the heart belongs.

Our family is our gift from God. One person can make such a difference in your life by one thoughtful act or encouraging word. Things happen sometimes allowing things to fall into place naturally.

Have you ever taken the time to have a hot bath? It does wonders for you. Feel joy. Every experience in life is a lesson, learn from it. Ask yourself about things you need to change in your life. You have the preference or priority in any decision. There are new ways to look at situations. Forgive yourself. Ego is blinding it.

Do you think there is a little bit of "Cinderella" in every woman? Deep soul searching reveals true emotion ultimately. You'll feel free and happy. Perhaps it's time for "out with the old in with the new" though some traditions are sacred.

Are you vulnerable to a person with a strong "control freak" attitude? Dictate your own life as a mission with sympathy and understanding and happiness in a worthy goal. It does wonders for your soul.

Have you ever noticed with your children that sometimes whatever they loved when they were little carried through to their adulthood? Think about yourself and what you love to do. I know how Bob loved his veggie garden. You could say our family loves the outdoors.

Our Father, who art in heaven, hallowed be Thy name. Thy kingdom come. Thy will be done on earth, as it is in heaven. Give us this day our daily bread. And forgive us our debts, as we forgive our debtors. And lead us not into temptation, but deliver us from evil. For Thine is the kingdom, and the power, and the glory, forever. Amen.

FAMILY AND FRIENDS

Dear God,

Autumn, nature's final blaze of glory! Apples, pumpkins, mums, and Halloween! Leaves everywhere! We're so lucky to have four seasons. I love that. Don't you love the smell of bacon frying or coffee perking? These seasonal changes affect me with feelings of joy to be alive. I'm so grateful to God for this enjoyment. I feel renewed.

Being in this choir is a blessing. Each one of you is so wonderful. As for our Karen—she is amazing. I thank each one of you for your love and friendship. I know that God has taken me from hunger to happiness here with you. Life goes on.

As parents, we always want the best for our children. When they amaze us with becoming exceptional adults, we can feel we've done well. Thank You, God. Do you feel a smile in your heart at times? Often the vigorous pursuit of success is from the way you were raised in childhood by an example set by your father or mother. Some futures are dictated by who we are, as opposed to what we want. So is status. What is more important than the feeling of love? In our needs and endeavors, we all need kind words and encouragement. We make mistakes. We need to love and to be happy. It's that simple.

Harmony is key in relationships. At times being a listening friend is the answer. True friends are always there for you providing love and comfort. There are no replacements for them. They make time for you. It's not easy to see another person's side of an issue. Have flexibility. It's a great day when you realize that your job and career aren't enough for your life. When you reach

214

a point of having love, a home, and family, that's a real life. That's a full life with God.

Our Father, who art in heaven, hallowed be Thy name. Thy kingdom come. Thy will be done on earth, as it is in heaven. Give us this day our daily bread. And forgive us our debts, as we forgive our debtors. And lead us not into temptation, but deliver us from evil. For Thine is the kingdom, and the power, and the glory, forever. Amen.

FAMILY AND FRIENDS

Dear God,

I'm so blessed to be in America! I love this place! Every trip or journey you take becomes a memory. Visiting an old hang-out or seeing friends seldom seen brings a new joy to your life. Do you have a spot in your home that gives you the greatest happy peace and comfort? It really does wonders for your whole being.

When you find God, your personality improves. Stepping out of one life into another one here made me realize so many things. Your money, the word "insurance" and supermarkets totally put me in shock!! It was challenging! I have to admit, I still don't understand insurance and I still am awed at Stop & Shop! I'm still working at it after so many mistakes! I just laugh at myself. There are more important things than money.

When there's upsetting news, don't withhold it. Deal with it even though motherly advice isn't always welcomed! The things we do for our children, either when they show promise or talent, we want them to fulfill themselves and be responsible. It could be their future vocation. We all question the paths we choose and what we accomplish in life, so reach out to your children with love and respect and grace and calm with your breadth of years of experience and maturity.

It's not easy to take a stand, but as parents we can blow away the hurt and fear experienced by our children. It's a mother's love! Give a hug and say "I love you." What does that mean exactly if your actions say something otherwise? Love demands a notion of sacrifice and love should always come first.

Our Father, who art in heaven, hallowed be Thy name. Thy kingdom come. Thy will be done on earth, as it is in heaven. Give us this day our daily bread. And forgive us our debts, as we forgive our debtors. And lead us not into temptation, but deliver us from evil. For Thine is the kingdom, and the power, and the glory, forever. Amen.

FAMILY AND FRIENDS

Dear God,

It only takes a moment to give a warm greeting, to enjoy the smell of lilacs or a rose, or to feel joy in simple things like laughter, friends, family and children, the joy of music, the sunshine of a smile, a short nap or a hand to hold. Also a restful night's sleep!

To have a friend who senses what you never say, but comforts you by just being there. I can only control what I do each moment, right now, to be better and grateful is exceptional. Our choices decide who we are but our love defines who we'll become.

You all have special memories through the years. Memories stored in your heart that you can recall at a moment's notice remain forever. The passing down of memories is a strong link that binds a family or friends. For what we hold in our hearts is one component of our humanity. Our family is a gift from You, God. Only You look down and send us sunshine. You smooth our pathways and dry our tears. Your saving grace reminds us to reach out to others with love, honesty, and kindness. Each day is a treasure and where there is love, there is a smile.

Our Father, who art in heaven, hallowed be Thy name. Thy kingdom come. Thy will be done on earth, as it is in heaven. Give us this day our daily bread. And forgive us our debts, as we forgive our debtors. And lead us not into temptation, but deliver us from evil. For Thine is the kingdom, and the power, and the glory, forever. Amen.

FAMILY AND FRIENDS

Dear God,

Within a family at a time of death and loss, I have felt and seen emotions of greed and self-entitlement and arguments over contents. That's so sad! Even though Bob's mother was living with us, some family members came and thoroughly stripped us of all the valuables. Bob and I were satisfied that we bought the house, not its contents. And because he married me, what was important to us was that some of the family accepted me and to this day I'm very close to my sister-in-law and many family members.

It was a huge challenge for me, living every day with hate from Bob's mom and serving her meals with no conversation. Thank God for Bob! Coming from my background it was a total shock. My older sister was always on the "Best Dressed" list in Shanghai, secretary to the Consul General at the Embassy where my Dad was the Attorney General. We always had two servants living with us. Thank God, I could laugh about the situation. Humor triumphs over anger.

Sometimes it takes time to stand up for our beliefs. Have affection and warmth for people and enjoy them. Have love and respect for yourself and others. Don't be a prisoner to defensiveness. It only builds a wall in your persona. Have a great sense of awareness and have hope and a free spirit.

Pay attention to the little things in life because they stay forever. Stay close to the ones you love with all your heart. Isn't it wonderful that all we have to do is ask God and believe that He can give us hope in place of doubt, and love and peace of mind in place of fear? Feel His touch and thank Him.

Our Father, who art in heaven, hallowed be Thy name. Thy kingdom come. Thy will be done on earth, as it is in heaven. Give us this day our daily bread. And forgive us our debts, as we forgive our debtors. And lead us not into temptation, but deliver us from evil. For Thine is the kingdom, and the power, and the glory, forever. Amen.

FAMILY AND FRIENDS

Dear God,

Thank you for letting me be like a "comfort blanket" to my children; also, to live in freedom instead of fear is a gift I'll cherish forever. Time spent with loved ones enjoying friendly chats is the time of my life in spite of "senior" moments!

Enjoy reading books. It gives you quiet peace for your soul. Are you a person who is fierce in your convictions even when others disagree with you? We all have minds of our own even if we don't have all the answers to many things. Aren't we always making choices? Sometimes we need our bravado renewed.

The definition of a true friend is one who senses what you want to say when you don't. Even though we take different paths, we take a little of each other with us. Life goes on. We need to find our niche. Copping out of a situation doesn't always save it until you let it go. Will you find the peace you deserve? Not all things are black or white. Criticism is a bitter pill to swallow. Do you know someone who has an answer for everything? We all have felt guilty about something we did or said sometime. Be honest with yourself and enjoy quality time a day at a time. If you do, you will feel peace and be a different person.

Decisions are not simple. Do you feel a sense of permanency within your home? You should! Enjoy love, joy, happiness, sadness, and a lifetime of sweet tomorrows. There are many people successful in their careers and still have an unhappy home. So make your life a growing experience. The choices are yours to make. Give a hug that's warm. Feel love. It will give you the resilience for every day. With God extraordinary things happen at times where people never expect it.

Our Father, who art in heaven, hallowed be Thy name. Thy kingdom come. Thy will be done on earth, as it is in heaven. Give us this day our daily bread. And forgive us our debts, as we forgive our debtors. And lead us not into temptation, but deliver us from evil. For Thine is the kingdom, and the power, and the glory, forever. Amen.

FAMILY AND FRIENDS

Dear God,

Thank you for giving me deep appreciation and understanding for friends and loved ones. It puts a spark into my life. Sharing is good for the soul. Each one of us has many facets to our persona. Dealing with people every day, do you do it with ease? It's so important to do it with honesty and love.

Welcome to old age when answers to a question can be answered 30 minutes later. It's wonderful that we can go where we want to and do what we want to do. Enjoy memory-making family occasions! Be flexible. Your eyes reflect your happiness if your heart is happy. Have a passion for life every day. Sometimes within a family there can be a failure of connection and warmth. It happens. Bob helped me through my tough patches with a simple hug. God's spirit was there.

Ideas and decisions say plenty about an individual. Trust your instinct in doing the right thing. Trust the person who you are. Share each day with hope and love with everyone. In relationships encouragement should always be a part of the comfort given to each other. Bob was so good about that.

It's amazing how some little things that happened in your life still matter years later. The feeling of great, deep familiarity with some friends or family and your home is truly one of the best gifts you could receive and enjoy within your life. The simplicity of the events in your day can give you such happiness. Life is for living. Only as we leave things behind in the past, do we move forward positively every day. Are you satisfied with who you are and what you are?

Our Father, Who art in heaven, hallowed by Thy name. Thy kingdom come. Thy will be done on earth as it is in heaven. Give us this day our daily bread. And forgive us our debts, as we forgive our debtors. And lead us not into temptation, but deliver us from evil. For Thine is the kingdom and the power, and the glory, forever. Amen.

FAMILY AND FRIENDS

Dear God,

This church is not a monument, it's a movement! God has given us each other so we are not alone. Only friends will tell you the truths you need to hear to make your life bearable. Happiness in ourselves is so important because we don't get to choose how we're going to die, or when. You can only decide how you're going to live now.

Put up with the rain if you want to see a rainbow. It's never too late to be what you want to be with honesty, compassion and kindness. What we hold in our hearts is truly the strongest component of our humanity. The saddest people in life are the ones who don't care deeply about anything. Have passion and satisfaction; they go hand in hand to create happiness.

Do you feel someone else's happiness at times? It should be infectious. Remember, your heart and mind must be in harmony. Do you ever think that your mind is like a light in the house? It's far reaching in warmth and encompasses everything. See into life, don't just look at it. Love unconditionally because God does. Each one's happiness is important. Have an inner core of strength and be a survivor.

Thank You, God, for always being there for me, making my life so worthwhile. I feel joy in the newness of each day. Set your own pace. Your character is your destiny. Love your children and teach them to care for others. Weren't bath times and bedtime stories the best times? Their smiles were priceless. That is a memory of love.

Our Father, who art in heaven, hallowed be Thy name. Thy kingdom come. Thy will be done on earth, as it is in heaven. Give us this day our daily bread. And forgive us our debts, as we forgive our debtors. And lead us not into temptation, but deliver us from evil. For Thine is the kingdom, and the power, and the glory, forever. Amen.

FAMILY AND FRIENDS

Dear God,

The breathlessness of winter brings a ballet of snowflakes, snow balls and snowmen, ice-skates and sleds. With trees covered in white ermine fur, it's a beautiful scene to behold, making shoveling a boring chore.

Have you ever felt "spiritual power" move you in some profound way? That's a God moment. Respect your past and never forget it, but always remember you can't live there!! When problems occur, sometimes the answer has been sitting right in front of you the whole time. So talk about it, pray about it, know your strengths and your weaknesses, and feel God's love!

Never let me get so busy that I can't find time for others, friendships, family and relationships because they are essential components to a happy life. We do have to cross that bridge when we come to it, especially when going through a tough time.

When you look at your life honestly, do you have any regrets? I know I have, I wish I had seen my Dad more! Life doesn't come with time for us to be "prepared" for action, so lean on God, feel His answer. As parents we have to have believe in ourselves first, as many things don't work out as planned.

Do you say, "I can't do it," or do you say, "I won't do it?" There's a huge difference in attitude and result. Have you noticed that certain things or certain people stay in your life forever? Special moments spent with your children are remembrances like a favorite song with feeling. We need people with more heart. Best friends are your soul mates! They have been there with you through every triumph and tragedy that has shaped your life. You are blessed. Those friends and God shine like a bright light from within you.

Our Father, who art in heaven, hallowed be Thy name. Thy kingdom come. Thy will be done on earth, as it is in heaven. Give us this day our daily bread. And forgive us our debts, as we forgive our debtors. And lead us not into temptation, but deliver us from evil. For Thine is the kingdom, and the power, and the glory, forever. Amen.

FAMILY AND FRIENDS

Dear God,

There is no time like the present. There is joy in living and in embracing life's journey. Think of a "special moment" in your life, a joy that brings a tear to your eyes. Quiet times spent with God lift my spirit. Have a heart that takes what comes each day. God will help you through your of burdens of disappointment, loneliness, annoyances, aches and pain. Hold His hand and find something enjoyable in any situation.

God's love is forever. Have you ever thought about the gift of your children? Have you ever thought about the bright moments with your son or daughter? They are precious, rewarding, humorous, and loving. You raised them. They fill our inner being of love. They give us a purpose in life. They touch our lives in so many ways. Without them life would be empty and unfulfilling. In time they move on with their lives and give us another dimension and extension of our love. The visits, phone calls, hugs and kisses, smiles, joy, and laughter are all a recipe we all enjoy!!

Life is good and you will feel that contentment if you take the time to reflect on your own life and blessings. I've come a long way for a girl who was shy and never opened her mouth for years. I'm standing and praying.

Our Father, who art in heaven, hallowed be Thy name. Thy kingdom come. Thy will be done on earth, as it is in heaven. Give us this day our daily bread. And forgive us our debts, as we forgive our debtors. And lead us not into temptation, but deliver us from evil. For Thine is the kingdom, and the power, and the glory, forever. Amen.

FAMILY AND FRIENDS

Dear God,

I love starting my day with You. You remind me that I was blessed to be married to an extraordinary man with a spiritual nature, and to share our life together. His thoughtfulness, kindness and calmness when I was upset was a true gift. Never forget to remind someone how important they are to you and that they make a difference in your life. Positive energy adds pleasure to basic life.

Use common sense, the necessary ingredient for our ups and downs. Embrace God. Relationships and friendships that have survived over time are made better with age because it builds trust.

Have you ever felt anxious and doubtful inwardly, but still went about your day with sheer will and poise? Lean on God, and be gentle with yourself. If you do, life will be so much happier and enjoyable. Hold that thought, then smile with that warmth.

Intuition is a powerful vehicle in life. We've all had "gut" feelings about people and things. Do you feel there is "depth" in your life? Be generous with your time, you will be blessed beyond expectation.

Thank you, Carol, for cleaning my robe. I thank you for making me feel loved. I feel God's spirit in your presence. You are so special as individuals and as a group. Words are inadequate to the feelings of my heart. To top it all, we make beautiful music together under Karen's tutelage. God is smiling! Let us age together, happy to be singing, praying, and enjoying each other's lives.

Our Father, who art in heaven, hallowed be Thy name. Thy kingdom come. Thy will be done on earth, as it is in heaven. Give us this day our daily bread. And forgive us our debts, as we forgive our debtors. And lead us not into temptation, but deliver us from evil. For Thine is the kingdom, and the power, and the glory, forever. Amen.

FAMILY AND FRIENDS

Dear God,

Thank You for honest relationships and worthwhile people with similar values. We all have to accept responsibility for our actions and be capable of mature judgments by not blaming others, but by taking responsibility for ourselves. Do you know someone who always makes people feel better about themselves and life in general? That's a blessing!

Our grandchildren live in a "tech" life as we try to age gracefully by writing "to do" lists, checking the obituaries, and finding an answer to a question of a name or place 30 minutes later!! I do laugh at myself many times a day!! Do you think there are exceptions to a rule? Demands of your job give you less time to dwell on your problems. Some people develop a quiet dignity in spite of the struggle. Do you have a least favorite day of the week? For some reason, I don't like Mondays.

Do you remember how you felt when you sent your first child off to school? That's a "wow" moment. I hope your home gives you a sense of safety and happiness. It's so great to have a home and feel the love of your family. Life is long lived for some. Sadly it's short for some. Parenthood has no expiration date.

We always thought it was better to do one thing at a time. Today people multitask more often than not. Humor can save us through a difficult time. Believe in yourself. Have you ever felt a failure as a mother? Learn to forgive yourself. Life isn't about what happens to you; it's about how you handle it. As each day passes, we have to make choices. Find ways to keep living. It's amazing what we all do for love. Having a family is the sweetest treasure on earth, and having God in your life gives you solid, untold joy.

Our Father, who art in heaven, hallowed be Thy name. Thy kingdom come. Thy will be done on earth, as it is in heaven. Give us this day our daily bread. And forgive us our debts, as we forgive our debtors. And lead us not into temptation, but deliver us from evil. For Thine is the kingdom, and the power, and the glory, forever. Amen.

FAMILY AND FRIENDS

Dear God,

Today I'm remembering my father's love. It always touched me. Every Saturday, after eating breakfast together, he'd sit me on his lap and want to know how my week went, and he would ask me if I had any needs, and then he'd give me my pocket money. I needed new shoes once, and he immediately said, "I will take you downtown to get them, and then we'll go for waffles at a tea room." I love waffles. It was my alone time with him. He listened to me and hugged me.

I knew I would never see my father again when I left Shanghai, and that is a sad memory for me. He didn't want to come to America because being the Attorney General for the Embassy of Portugal, he travelled extensively. He substituted for the Consul General often. I'm sure he taught me about life's injustices, love and kindness.

As parents, reach out to your children because it remains for life a mainstay of love, a treasure and gift to keep. Do you like to get up close and comfortable with people? I do. I love people. Happiness is not in just having or receiving, it's also about giving. Where love is, God is.

Remember building sand castles on the beach or feeding ducks at a pond with your children? You are the architect of your own life. Think long and hard about this journey. Be honest and kind to yourself. God will help you. Have thoughts that count. Help the less fortunate. Make the world a better place even if it's in a small way. You will feel loved and blessed.

Our Father, who art in heaven, hallowed be Thy name. Thy kingdom come. Thy will be done on earth, as it is in heaven. Give us this day our daily bread. And forgive us our debts, as we forgive our debtors. And lead us not into temptation, but deliver us from evil. For Thine is the kingdom, and the power, and the glory, forever. Amen.

FAMILY AND FRIENDS

Dear God,

Thanksgiving! I had never heard of it until I came to America, and now it's one of my favorite days. It has so much meaning to me! Happy moments to share with family and friends can never be taken away. It reminds me how blessed I am to be alive and present to celebrate it. Have you ever helped someone and felt in your head and whole being that it was right? That's God's Thanksgiving.

Do you ever stop to think about the changes that have occurred in your life? Were there some you never anticipated? I've learned that the attitude of your mind every day is so important because it affects your whole being. It's not always easy to accept people for who they are and what they do. Do you live your life by a code of ethics? And would you ever compromise your responsibility?

The path of life is about looking inwardly at yourself in order to love yourself. Be honest about it. Have respect for people around you, and also for yourself. Love life, have a sense of humor—we only live once.

Have you ever met someone who is like a breath of fresh air? A person with a heart of gold? The expression on your face divulges your feelings in life within a situation. Confrontation with a person or family member is difficult, but it happens. Take God's hand, He will give you the strength to deal with it. Laugh at yourself when you fall short because we all make mistakes. Acceptance is a good thing.

Don't you love people who are honest, loving and faithful? Thank You for Bob's love and hugs. It's great to be on the same page with someone who has the same spirit given what time we have left in this world. Each day and moment is a treasure, it's more valuable than gold. With love comes quiet peace.

Our Father, who art in heaven, hallowed be Thy name. Thy kingdom come. Thy will be done on earth, as it is in heaven. Give us this day our daily bread. And forgive us our debts, as we forgive our debtors. And lead us not into temptation, but deliver us from evil. For Thine is the kingdom, and the power, and the glory, forever. Amen.

FAMILY AND FRIENDS

Dear God,

Thank You for miracles that happen in a person's life. They really hit us at times, or they come disguised. Have you ever had a day in your life from the first instance, you knew it was going to be a "Red Letter" day? It can be good or bad. Even with interruptions, a family can remain a family. Some people handle responsibility at work magnificently, but when it comes to their own home they don't seem to pitch in, nor think that it's necessary. That's a huge cut off because it's important to have responsibility in both areas.

Do you think that the words strength, hope, joy and love are essential feelings that give us peace of mind? I know I couldn't live without them. Be present for your family and friends. Tomorrows can't be relied upon; we only have today. So feel love for someone, and it will fill your heart with joy and give you the warmth for life. In spite of grief, remember the good things to propel yourself forward to feel love and laughter again.

Are you so settled in your ways that you can't deal with change? Remember a friend of your heart is such a blessing. They share their love for you lessening your worries and doubling up your joy to live and carry on. Facing reality isn't the easiest lesson for most of us to learn. We all need to lighten up on things we've been so rigid about. It can be a "magic-carpet" moment.

By reflecting on your attitude, you will discover many meaningful truths about yourself. We were all raised a certain way, to think and react a certain way. It's up to us to pick that which we think will make a difference for our lives. Life is so valuable so love each day and enjoy it.

238

Are you happy with the person you are? Inward happiness radiates out to others. When trouble comes and your heart is breaking and tears start to fall, God will always be there to comfort you and give you strength. Rest in His love, He holds the key to your life. Know what you believe in, have a sense of joyful rejoicing, and don't waste a precious day. Be a lover of life.

Our Father, who art in heaven, hallowed be Thy name. Thy kingdom come. Thy will be done on earth, as it is in heaven. Give us this day our daily bread. And forgive us our debts, as we forgive our debtors. And lead us not into temptation, but deliver us from evil. For Thine is the kingdom, and the power, and the glory, forever. Amen.

FAMILY AND FRIENDS

Dear God,

I'm thinking about some of the friends I have. They bring me tears of happiness. Do you have a friend who is an absolute treasure? Is your friend someone thoughtful and kind who helps you discover your real self? That's a blessing.

Communicate and deal with upsets or else they will eat at your inner being and affect your health. Timing is everything. Have you ever met someone and just loved that person right away? I have many times. It's a celebration for me! Pass on your wisdom. You have much to offer even though all of us have made many mistakes. Allow forgiveness for yourself and move forward with your life.

Sudden death is always a shock, but in time you realize you have to carry on with an incentive for life. The person's spirit will always be with you surrounded by God's love. Know who you are. Be real. Life is full of successes. Don't disappoint yourself. We all have certain standards we live up to. Be enthusiastic about it. Try to fulfill some of your dreams. It can be rewarding. God sends the sun up every day. Realize the depth of your life even as you age. Things don't have to be perfect. You still make mistakes. Enjoy love, family, and every day. The list is like an endless Thanksgiving parade.

Each one of us is special. Know what you want and believe in yourself even if you lack self-confidence. Achievement will restore it. Years later have you wondered if you made the right decisions for yourself or your children? You'll know you're happy when you can feel a smile inside of you. Your choice of friends can reveal your needs in addition to enjoying their company. Music and love add to your welfare.

Our Father, who art in heaven, hallowed be Thy name. Thy kingdom come. Thy will be done on earth, as it is in heaven. Give us this day our daily bread. And forgive us our debts, as we forgive our debtors. And lead us not into temptation, but deliver us from evil. For Thine is the kingdom, and the power, and the glory, forever. Amen.

FAMILY AND FRIENDS

Dear God,

Thank You for letting me realize when someone becomes an essential part of my life when their absence is felt. As children get older moments spent with them lessen. However, the thought of them blossoming in their lives is a blessing of God's grace.

Make a day valuable by planning a special time with someone you love. Celebrate their thoughtfulness and laugh. Friends and family are your heart's companion. Try to live each day as a new adventure. Some people in life are "keepers" forever. You never know when a smile or a hello can change your life. Just holding someone's hand is so meaningful it calms you if you're upset. It reassures you of love.

Discover your true selves in life's journey—values, grateful friends, precious time, and God's blessings. We are what we do and say, not what we intend to do or not do. With God's help, it happens, one hurdle at a time. Life changes and happiness is possible. There are silver linings. No one can do it for you. Good guys do win, and love builds bridges. Genuine affection in relationships is a key in life.

Do you notice how drama follows some people throughout their lives? They often instill on themselves their hurt and pain, and an endless string of the same mistakes. Their plateau remains the same, instead of moving forward to a better life. It's there for the taking, even when we've reached our limit.

Are you worrying about your next phase of life? Or are you just glad to be alive? Remember things can get better instead of worse. If you're lucky, you'll fill that empty space with someone special who makes you smile. We all have to make choices—choices that touch our hearts.

Our Father, who art in heaven, hallowed be Thy name. Thy kingdom come. Thy will be done on earth, as it is in heaven. Give us this day our daily bread. And forgive us our debts, as we forgive our debtors. And lead us not into temptation, but deliver us from evil. For Thine is the kingdom, and the power, and the glory, forever. Amen.

FAMILY AND FRIENDS

Dear God,

How long does it take us to realize that we need to make room for You in our lives? Every day You give us a sunrise and sunset, the stars and the moon to light our way, rain and snow to cover our earth. It's all a miracle!

It's a blessing to have a friend who gives us joy or to be a good listener when needed. Sometimes that's all it takes to give a fresh start to a person or to yourself. Always remember what the heart has loved most will never be lost.

Spend time with those you love best. Walk or bike in happiness, absorbing everything around you. It's reflecting God's love for you.

Live wisely, you are God's creation, for tomorrow is a mystery. Each of us must have a dream. We won't lose if we try and fail. We do lose if we don't try. Believe in yourself by keeping God in sight. Life is more worthwhile when kindness, courage, love, and faith are woven in.

Thank You, God, for this wonderful group shining with Your spirit every day. I never cease to marvel at them. I love them for they are my extended family.

Our Father, who art in heaven, hallowed be Thy name. Thy kingdom come. Thy will be done on earth, as it is in heaven. Give us this day our daily bread. And forgive us our debts, as we forgive our debtors. And lead us not into temptation, but deliver us from evil. For Thine is the kingdom, and the power, and the glory, forever. Amen.

FAMILY AND FRIENDS

Dear God,

In today's world, having a sense of community is important. Celebrate friendship. It gives you a great feeling of peace. Have you known someone who was possibly a saint, always cheerful and thoughtful no matter what? Each of us has our own personality, and we are known by it even if we are very private. The month of May is a magical month! Remember God has plans for you, miracles happen. Some couples never tire of each other's company, but we all need a sprinkle of magic in our lives to reenergize!

Is there a special place you go to that recharges your batteries? Body language alone is enough to clue people whether you're a happy camper or not. Try to be one of the "good guys" in life. Are you interested in everyone and everything or do you start your day with no plans?

Some days are full of choices. Problems don't solve themselves neatly; they're solved by decisions. Be your own person! Can you walk away from your job if you hate it? Don't waste your life if your heart isn't in it!

Inner peace is important to our well-being. Your spirit can be reflected in a room, or your home, or yard. You have to be yourself, settled in your niche. You have to look out for yourself for no one else will. We are blessed when we have a special friend who is ours forever. That friend always has the time to be there with comfort and gives new meaning to everything. That special friend senses what you don't say and loves you in spite of what you lack. And her face and voice are gifts that are irreplaceable. Does that scenario remind you of God?

Our Father, who art in heaven, hallowed be Thy name. Thy kingdom come. Thy will be done on earth, as it is in heaven. Give us this day our daily bread. And forgive us our debts, as we forgive our debtors. And lead us not into temptation, but deliver us from evil. For Thine is the kingdom, and the power, and the glory, forever. Amen.

FAMILY AND FRIENDS

Dear God,

This morning my first thoughts were of You and Your gifts to us. Forgiveness, Your strength for our trials and tasks, happiness even in sorrow, and Your love. This moment belongs only to You and me.

We are all someone. You could have a college degree or be an athlete, but without friends, you have nothing. We all feel tremulous about attempting a new career or something new. Have you been in a moment when the air is filled with questions you didn't ask? Or have you ever felt uncertain and lacked the courage to let your real friend into your feelings? We have "real friends" and also "just friends." Real friends see us when we fall apart, when our world has stopped for a minute. They are the nearest and dearest!! They share their strength and unconditional love with support and honesty.

Look into a person's eyes. Eyes have a language all their own. They speak the truth. By living a happy life you live more. Choose your path. There's beauty within each one of us. Take time to read, remembering what your heart loved most. Love changes everything in what we do or say. Set the tempo. For each of us there is a reason why we live on the earth. Don't miss a blessing right before your eyes.

Sit with a grandchild. Remember a father's love. Celebrate the joy we find in music. Yesterdays are gone and tomorrow is still a mystery. So be a giver of hugs, smiles and kind thoughts.

Our Father, who art in heaven, hallowed be Thy name. Thy kingdom come. Thy will be done on earth, as it is in heaven.

Give us this day our daily bread. And forgive us our debts, as we forgive our debtors. And lead us not into temptation, but deliver us from evil. For Thine is the kingdom, and the power, and the glory, forever. Amen.

FAMILY AND FRIENDS

Dear God,

Here we are starting a New Year. Thank You! Enjoying Christmas makes us realize that what matters most aren't the traditions but what underpins them—love, devotion between family and friends, and also between generations. These things bind us together.

We first experience and give love in our family. It's also where we first experience rejection. Love can overcome the most painful rejection, and give you strength to put up with things we never should have to endure.

No moments spent loving someone are ever wasted. Having parents who love each other gives a child a sense of security. Love comes into your life at its own time, not when you're ready. When you lose someone you love, just taking one step at a time to deal with it eventually puts you in another place. Some of it is familiar, and some of it is not, but you make something else out of it, in spite of the loss.

Many times a kindness appears like a lifeline! You can have order and purpose in your life, but leave space for things to look forward to—unexpected rewards. At Christmas we celebrate Jesus' birth. Remember the birth of your own baby also. Wasn't that emotion so intense, filled with love and protectiveness, that it transformed you into a mother? Listen to your heart and reach out to your children as parents or grandparents.

Our Father, who art in heaven, hallowed be Thy name. Thy kingdom come. Thy will be done on earth, as it is in heaven. Give us this day our daily bread. And forgive us our debts, as we

forgive our debtors. And lead us not into temptation, but deliver us from evil. For Thine is the kingdom, and the power, and the glory, forever. Amen.

GUIDANCE

Dear God,

The sun is shining, and that alone gives me joy in starting a day. Everything in life is enjoyed more when it's shared. I love my quiet times with You and my thoughts. Isn't it great that we can live through wintry storms and enjoy the beauty of spring? The promise of a new day is a gift from God. Thank You.

What your heart has loved most is never lost. It can bring a smile to your face. Love gives you quiet peace. It's so important to feel love surrounding you. Share it. Take time to say, "I love you." Find joy in music. Feel the good things that happened to you today—a smile or lunch with a friend. It restores your hope and love. Life is full of changes and new chapters. Live them with enjoyment.

In this "tech" generation I still love the personal touch in life and letting people know how much I love them. You may have many friends, but only some wiggle their way into your heart to stay forever. You may not even get to spend time with them, but that special love remains.

We all need happenings in our life to stir our souls and touch our hearts. An open heart gives us the strength to face our own dilemmas. It's that simple! You know yourself and what you have gone through to survive. It changes your persona. With God you will feel so-o-o good. Believe that the best is yet to come. Your spirit will be renewed. Life is good.

Every day feel love, friendship, and appreciation. Your eyes will reflect God's love. It's good to laugh away our frustrations at times. Do you think that sorrows in our life bring us to connections with others? So feel the peace in your heart, and feel the joy in the simplicity of living every day. God's gift to us is every day's sunrise.

Our Father, who art in heaven, hallowed be Thy name. Thy kingdom come. Thy will be done on earth, as it is in heaven. Give us this day our daily bread. And forgive us our debts, as we forgive our debtors. And lead us not into temptation, but deliver us from evil. For Thine is the kingdom, and the power, and the glory, forever. Amen.

GUIDANCE

Dear God,

After marriage my generation generally stayed home and took care of the children and home. There wasn't a job we had to go to. We enjoyed the feeling of belonging and everything that the word "mother" entailed. When you commit to anything, do everything to make it work. I'm sure we wished for some down time many times.

Have you ever had a gut feeling about a person who is lying to you? Our children certainly kept us busy on that score. Listen to your heart. Trust yourself. Meet new people. You never know how enjoyable it can be to widen your circle of friends. Verbal conversation is so important. When you love someone, your eyes become gentle. Share ideas, opinions, and hopes. Do things from your heart. Pray to God in honesty. Enjoy the sun and nature and sense everything. Life demands so many things. Friends and family help in the depth of this prize.

Are you a people person? A resume isn't worth anything if you're unhappy at your job. For a change reward yourself by not having thoughts of "need" but of what "I want" instead. Be energized. Smile. Don't be selfish in life. Learn to compromise. It will give you a new dimension in life. Don't be a person married to your career, your pets, or sport. It can ruin a relationship. It's not easy to embrace change; however, it can be the best thing that ever happened to you. Seize the moment.

Each of us should make the most of our lives with a best effort and the right mind set. Have a conscience about what you say, so you don't hurt someone else's feelings. Pay attention to little thoughtful things. They are more important than the big things because it's the little things that remain in your life of memories.

Our Father, who art in heaven, hallowed be Thy name. Thy kingdom come. Thy will be done on earth, as it is in heaven. Give us this day our daily bread. And forgive us our debts, as we forgive our debtors. And lead us not into temptation, but deliver us from evil. For Thine is the kingdom, and the power, and the glory, forever. Amen.

GUIDANCE

Dear God,

The passing down of memories provides a strong link that binds family and friends together. For what we hold in our hearts is one component of our humanity. We should conduct our life with honesty, love, kindness and compassion reaching out to others with all those feelings. Life holds so much beauty, bright moments, and many gifts. The reward is that feeling of contentment within us.

Ask for God's help. Be a creature of "impulse" at times. Don't be sarcastic. It only causes tears for someone and it hurts. Focus more on sensitivity and love. Have you ever just hummed or sung a song in contentment? Have you ever just stood, looking at the stars? Timing is everything. You have to hurt before you heal. Life is full of "chance." Determine your happiness, choose your attitude because there are some days that are just a "no go." We are all restored differently.

Laugh and be happy. Have a zest for life. Make your whole body smile. That alone will affect your mind and body and improve your health. Always remember that your mind and your heart must be in harmony to give you that happiness in life.

Our Father, who art in heaven, hallowed be Thy name. Thy kingdom come. Thy will be done on earth, as it is in heaven. Give us this day our daily bread. And forgive us our debts, as we forgive our debtors. And lead us not into temptation, but deliver us from evil. For Thine is the kingdom, and the power, and the glory, forever. Amen.

GUIDANCE

Dear God,

I have learned with deep conviction that the true wealth of this earth is the bond of love and friendship. Simple truths and honest values are some of life's comforts that fulfill you every day. Family ties or a simple smile or a hug do wonders for your inner being. Thank God, feel His love.

People get to know you by the way you live. Take care of your home and how you handle grief, anger and love. Don't let grief use you. Use your grief instead. It makes you a better person and a better mother. You earned it all!!

Remember God's compassion and companionship, they are valuable assets. Do you know someone whose DNA is gorgeous inside and out? We as parents have to teach our children to be generous, to believe in themselves, and to take risks because the real tragedy in life is not losing money, but losing trust and love. There's nothing wrong in showing your uniqueness to others.

Life provides us good and bad, dreams and reality, ordinary and spectacular. Time can make a difference inside and out. Don't be stubborn, try new endeavors. It will bring laughter to your soul. Make an enthusiastic effort to do it.

Growing up, have you looked pretty and smooth on the outside but inwardly still felt uncertain and shy? It's important to know who you are and where you're going. We shape our own life at our own pace!! Love yourself. Half of my life was lived in shyness. I was called "Miss Wallflower." No one wanted to date or dance with me. Look at me now! I'm standing in front of you and I dance every day!

Our Father, who art in heaven, hallowed be Thy name. Thy kingdom come. Thy will be done on earth, as it is in heaven. Give us this day our daily bread. And forgive us our debts, as we forgive our debtors. And lead us not into temptation, but deliver us from evil. For Thine is the kingdom, and the power, and the glory, forever. Amen.

GUIDANCE

Dear God,

Sometimes we get lost in thought and we miss the importance of a person crossing our path in life. Thoughts come and go, but that person may not. There's training for a job taken or a sport, but there is no training for being good parents. It's an advantage and comfort if you get along with your parents. It's a feeling of love. Most everyone experiences that. Believe in God and His love. Have a new beginning. I did! I can't express to you the happiness I feel every day I'm alive and well. It's precious.

Do you like the town you live in? I love Hanover and my home, family and friends. There's a quiet peace in my yard, and I love mowing my lawn! Try not to be negative or sarcastic, it hurts. Be honest with yourself; we need inner peace. Tension in our body gets communicated by our body language personally or outwardly. Remember people interpret things in different ways. Always have a "sympathy vote" for someone. Judge a situation first, before you leap into it. Life is solving one thing and moving on to the next.

Make sure that love exists in your life. You can't have joy without sorrow at our saddest moments. The moon and stars still come out—that's God reminding you He is there. So enjoy music and dance, it makes you feel upbeat and it lowers your stress level. Say "I love you" to the people you care for. You never know when the next opportunity is going to be. Look at life with humor and your attitude and feelings will change for the better.

Our outward journey in life determines who we become inwardly. Value your life, good and bad. The end result will be happiness and love that fills your heart. Thank God for all of it.

Our Father, who art in heaven, hallowed be Thy name. Thy kingdom come. Thy will be done on earth, as it is in heaven. Give us this day our daily bread. And forgive us our debts, as we forgive our debtors. And lead us not into temptation, but deliver us from evil. For Thine is the kingdom, and the power, and the glory, forever. Amen.

GUIDANCE

Dear God,

Here we are going through Lent again. It's a time to look inwardly. Thank You for Karen's Musical Meditations which help me to discover my feelings at that moment. With eyes closed and ears opened, I felt peace and joy spread through my whole body making room in my heart for God. It's wonderful to feel a sense of belonging within yourself.

Have you ever felt your heart singing over something that happened in your life? I have. This year, 2015, my sister actually wrote to me to wish me "Happy Birthday" for the first time in over 40 years. I always kept in touch with her. I respected her decision to cut off the whole family because of the war and I did not contact her three sons. Her letter was over two pages long. Miracles do happen.

Life isn't about just money. Love is. Money comes and goes. Real love is forever. It's a doorway to caring and sharing simple little things like joy in a home, real friendships, and kindness for others.

We all suffer in our own way. It's so amazing how much we can endure and still survive. We all deserve that chance. Do you think parenthood teaches us how to hold it together in a crisis?

We are never prepared to lose someone we love. Feeling the grief of little things still brings tears, but with God's help we move forward.

Life is precious, so live it with passion, with energy and enthusiasm. Enjoy the beauty of sunshine, a hug and kiss from your daughter, a moment of laughter with a friend, feeling loved. Happiness is a matter of choice. It's so important to have peace of mind because it affects the rhythm of your body. Lean on God.

Our Father, who art in heaven, hallowed be Thy name. Thy kingdom come. Thy will be done on earth, as it is in heaven. Give us this day our daily bread. And forgive us our debts, as we forgive our debtors. And lead us not into temptation, but deliver us from evil. For Thine is the kingdom, and the power, and the glory, forever. Amen.

GUIDANCE

Dear God,

Thank You for the sunshine. It always gives us the impetus to enjoy the day, puts us in a good mood, and recharges our energy.

Sometimes bad things happen in our life like pain, failure, loss. God is always there to help us rebuild our lives giving us a whole new way of dealing with our heartaches and joys. When you feel a gentle touch or a kiss on the cheek or receive a warm loving note from a friend, you know life is good!

We all need to see a rainbow. Be grateful and say "thank You" to God. I do that all the time and He blesses me. His gifts are free—from sunshine to moonlight. Make a quiet place for yourself. That's so important. Walk. Listen to children laugh and sing, jump and play. Don't ever get so busy you neglect those you love.

It's hard to be patient and to understand instead of feeling anger and losing hope. There are many honesties of life—simple truths —accept them. Have you ever looked at something or a place and remembered the sweet spirit of a person? That's a special kind of love, a special moment.

Our Father, who art in heaven, hallowed be Thy name. Thy kingdom come. Thy will be done on earth, as it is in heaven. Give us this day our daily bread. And forgive us our debts, as we forgive our debtors. And lead us not into temptation, but deliver us from evil. For Thine is the kingdom, and the power, and the glory, forever. Amen.

GUIDANCE

Dear God,

This morning is a beautiful day!! The sun is shining on a snow covered scene. Birds are chirping. The feeling is peaceful and it's joyful to be living in a great neighborhood with special people. Are you happy being yourself? Each of us came from somewhere. We hold onto things we love. Life can be as it is, but life can be as you make it. Ask for God's help.

Have you had to do something for the sake of your family even though you didn't like doing it? Being parents on the front line giving "the look" to your children takes respect and compassion. We have only one life so make sure it's a good one.

Pain in life makes us who we are. It teaches us or tames us; it destroys us or saves us. Some of it is of our own doing, but some of it is out of our control. It's important to feel "special" in a parent's eyes. It may be a long way to go with no map to get there. Sometimes a wound needs to be lanced or it festers. So try to dance through difficult times because happiness is a gift. Its warmth reminds us of beauty and goodness.

Feel the strength from God touching you. Never take it for granted. It's amazing what you can cope with when you need to. Laugh at yourself after an incident. It's such a good feeling. Make the world a funnier place. Be in the moment, one step at a time. Love what you're doing and let it mean something to you. Remember God's love. Feel it.

Our Father, who art in heaven, hallowed be Thy name. Thy kingdom come. Thy will be done on earth, as it is in heaven. Give us this day our daily bread. And forgive us our debts, as we

forgive our debtors. And lead us not into temptation, but deliver us from evil. For Thine is the kingdom, and the power, and the glory, forever. Amen.

GUIDANCE

Dear God,

It's been six years this May since Bob's death. The girls, grandchildren, and I go to Ogunquit every year to honor Bob by walking the "Marginal Way." We pray and toss roses into the ocean in thanks for all that he stood for and did and for his love and hugs. His heart was in the right place.

So I continue on, feeling joy in living, feeling his spirit surrounding me and the miracle of God. Live and love because those are the memories that will cover you like a warm cuddly blanket.

Look back over your life honestly. It opens up a whole vista of feelings and truths. Happiness only comes if you look inward at yourself. When you're faced with loneliness you have to dig in to develop yourself in so many ways positively.

With God we can develop and maintain an attitude of mind to deal with the daily circumstances in life. Do I stumble? Many, many times. However, I feel each day is so worthwhile. Never leave a kind word unspoken. Enjoy everything in bloom. See the chickadees, cardinals and robins. Hear the spring peepers. God's world can bring joy and life to our hearts.

Our Father, who art in heaven, hallowed be Thy name. Thy kingdom come. Thy will be done on earth, as it is in heaven. Give us this day our daily bread. And forgive us our debts, as we forgive our debtors. And lead us not into temptation, but deliver us from evil. For Thine is the kingdom, and the power, and the glory, forever. Amen.

GUIDANCE

Dear God,

Stress. I hear that word so often. Why do we allow that to happen to us? It's not worth it because it affects our health! We really need to work on that and defeat it. If we're honest about it we know that in our lives we have much more happiness and love than stress!!

So we need to keep God in sight and He will give us new strength and comfort to carry on. It can be life-changing! Try it, you'll like it! Every human life needs a spiritual dimension or it isn't a complete life. Do you think our spiritual beliefs influence our morality to a capacity? Little mistakes, day to day things, can be fatal if said or done in the wrong way.

There is always a new day and new life. Concentrate on happiness and laugh and enjoy it. After living through change and hurt, enjoy freedom and enjoy the partner you love. Happy people don't always have the best of everything. It's because they know how to survive through bad times and still come away singing and dancing! Spend time with optimistic people. It's good for your soul and mind.

Savor mid-life and older. They're wonderful years! It's your turn to enjoy life. Live with your heart, focus on your life, and you will feel energized. Enjoy quality time with your family. Remember life is simply a collection of years! Fill them with love, music, and art. Your heart's desires will fill with the zeal of a missionary. Make time for God and prayer. That is a recipe to mix and to keep.

Our Father, who art in heaven, hallowed be Thy name. Thy kingdom come. Thy will be done on earth, as it is in heaven. Give us this day our daily bread. And forgive us our debts, as we forgive our debtors. And lead us not into temptation, but deliver us from evil. For Thine is the kingdom, and the power, and the glory, forever. Amen.

GUIDANCE

Dear God,

I believe winter is here with snow hanging low on boughs. Evergreens are so lovely. A chill is in the air and everything is covered with a blanket of white. How do people manage heavy responsibilities if they haven't been raised that way? I'm sure some do magnificently, while some flounder. Have you ever done something in your past that can jump up and embarrass you in the present?

We all have a different point of view about life and happiness. Some situations can change your life forever. It's great to be busy doing things, but it's also nice to just relax. We need both in our lives. Don't you love to sit with the sun shining on your back? The warmth gives you a great feeling. Even cats and dogs enjoy that, too. There's nothing like the promise of a sunny day.

Life is all about happiness and laughter and sorrow and pain. Take God's hand, and He will give you inner joy. Be true to yourself. Do you know what you want out of life, and do you work at it every day? It takes confidence to achieve that. How have you lived your life so far? Is it a simple dictum of honesty and responsibility in spite of black or white choices or that gray area of choice?

I find that music alone can empty your mind in good times or bad. Stop worrying about what other people think about you. Worry more about what you want to do. You'll be so much happier in your life. Keep yourself grounded. There are many people who are so wrapped up in their own drama in life more times than not. So, thank You, God, for Your loving care and for always being there, and thank You for allowing me to experience a true love.

Our Father, who art in heaven, hallowed be Thy name. Thy kingdom come. Thy will be done on earth, as it is in heaven. Give us this day our daily bread. And forgive us our debts, as we forgive our debtors. And lead us not into temptation, but deliver us from evil. For Thine is the kingdom, and the power, and the glory, forever. Amen.

GUIDANCE

Dear God,

When trust is instilled between people, it will always be returned to you. The same will follow with joy! Remember to love God for His love and care. We have so many reasons to motivate ourselves and feel satisfied with kindness and love.

Don't you love fall with its colorful trees and mums? Don't you love the apples, pumpkins, and Halloween? It's important to have ambition! You need to be where you want to be and doing what you want to do. Some dreams do come true. Are you a person who refuses to take "no" for an answer?

Most parents try to teach their children about family, love, art, music and sports and know how to combine them into a happy, skillful endeavor. Looking inwardly at yourself honestly, can you admit that you reflect some of the upbringing of your parents? So know yourself better than any other person, even if you fail at times make your life feel worthy. Stress ages you so be kind to yourself. It helps you feel young. Life is precious.

When times are bad, try to focus on the good things in your life. It will remind you of your inner strength and love. Celebrate with it. Happiness affects your health. Have you ever stopped and felt so good in your heart that you know you did the right thing? That's a rich moment!! To have friends who are all that they are, sharing their love and kindness, leaves me with gratitude in my life.

Listen to your inner thoughts and feelings. You will see clarity. Don't forget that God opens doors when we think we can't. To have success in life we have to be thoughtful, dependable, and trustworthy. All of us live in a world with different parameters for our personal happiness. Some people can break your heart more than once, so look at the stars and moon and unburden yourself. Help comes in many ways.

Our Father, who art in heaven, hallowed be Thy name. Thy kingdom come. Thy will be done on earth, as it is in heaven. Give us this day our daily bread. And forgive us our debts, as we forgive our debtors. And lead us not into temptation, but deliver us from evil. For Thine is the kingdom, and the power, and the glory, forever. Amen.

OUTLOOK ON LIFE

Dear God,

Every day our lives are shaped by our loved ones and friends. As parents of children, we operate on instinct, hope, and fear. We even bend rules. You have a choice to forgive someone or something instead of holding resentment. Have you ever felt a love/hate relationship in your life about a person, job, or place? We all make mistakes when not thinking about risks being taken or rewards we gain as we seek happiness. Maintaining a balanced life is no easy task. Have you ever done the complete opposite of what you had logically thought about? Lean on God.

Summer is a time to be grateful and a time to take life easier. Smile and enjoy family and friends. Your eyes will reflect your contentment. You're lucky if you have a partner with humor and a big heart! Show enthusiasm in what you do. Be open to unexpected, delightful moments within your life. Singing in a choir with Karen's direction gives us unity that binds us together through lyrics, notes, and feelings.

Are you a warm and fuzzy person? All of us have different experiences and thoughts, but how we deal with them makes us who we are. Have you ever thought about how family and friends bind us together and give us a place on this earth? Some things in life stick with you forever. To this day, I love odd numbers and verandahs because the home I lost in the Japanese invasion was #9 Albury Lane and had a huge verandah running across the front of the upstairs. So think about your young life and see if you are partial to some things, too. It's a memory of the heart.

272

Take a deep breath and blow it out. Enjoy the beauty of a blue sky and beautiful clouds and the flowers and the birds. All of it is God's miracle for you. Feel God's hand touch you.

Our Father, who art in heaven, hallowed be Thy name. Thy kingdom come. Thy will be done on earth, as it is in heaven. Give us this day our daily bread. And forgive us our debts, as we forgive our debtors. And lead us not into temptation, but deliver us from evil. For Thine is the kingdom, and the power, and the glory, forever. Amen.

OUTLOOK ON LIFE

Dear God,

When things are going well in our journey of life, we feel confident as a person in the direction we're heading. Sometimes we must struggle and persist through tough times that bring us to where we belong. Being born in Shanghai, China, surviving the Japanese in World War II, helped me to adjust and adapt to America. What a great experience! Little things I never knew about like going to the beach just to hear the comforting sound of waves constantly lapping the beach were new to me. Now I love walking on the beach. Good things do happen in your life that are meant to be.

Things happen for a reason. I met Bob!! My life totally changed. Problems and worries are swept away in a night and can become the cares of yesterday if you greet a new day with God. We all suffer sometimes and need kindnesses because unpredictable events happen. You lose someone you love, but no matter what, their spirit stays with you.

Do you think that who we are and what we believe in comes from our past? Think about it!! For me I believe I am that person. It gave me a clear picture and motivation to strive for certain values because time does not stand still. I could not have accomplished it without God in my life, and praying for hours at a time. Life is so good, enjoy each day. I truly dance and sing like a nutcase every day around my kitchen in thankfulness to God.

Our Father, who art. in heaven, hallowed be Thy name. Thy kingdom come. Thy will be done on earth, as it is in heaven. Give us this day our daily bread. And forgive us our debts, as we

forgive our debtors. And lead us not into temptation, but deliver us from evil. For Thine is the kingdom, and the power, and the glory, forever. Amen.

OUTLOOK ON LIFE

Dear God,

It's such fun to go outdoors for a walk. All the tension and anxiety in your spirit that have been held, as if contained in a suitcase, get lifted out of your body.

Do you have a favorite holiday? Holidays are important. Easter is almost here so celebrate with the people you love. You never know when memories will be all that remain. Life is so precious. Celebrations are a bonus of love!

Does a person make your heart stutter? Love alone creates long-term thinking. That emotion is life affirming, invigorating and fun. As parents when we put two daughters or two sons together in a bedroom, those two siblings remain close all their lives. That is a blessing!

Believe in yourself. Have faith in God. Every day is a gift—a surprising phone call, a note, an invitation, sitting in the sanctuary listening to Karen play during "Musical Meditations" is a gift. It does wonders for our inner being. It unites all who love music and sustains us with a strong sense of deja-vu.

Sometimes things happen for a reason. Is it fate? Every journey has to end before we come home. It's lonely when you don't belong to someone. Give impulsive hugs. That's a good thing. During Lent every year I like to look inwardly at myself to be honest about my faults and errors, and ask God to help me to be a better person. It inspires me to try harder in my waltz through life.

Our Father, who art in heaven, hallowed be Thy name. Thy kingdom come. Thy will be done on earth, as it is in heaven. Give us this day our daily bread. And forgive us our debts, as we forgive our debtors. And lead us not into temptation, but deliver us from evil. For Thine is the kingdom, and the power, and the glory, forever. Amen.

OUTLOOK ON LIFE

Dear God,

I loved Chapin's sermon on a past Sunday. To climb up the corporate ladder till you reach the peak, then what? Knowledge is power and compelling when applied discreetly. Moving forward in anything you choose with confidence doesn't necessarily give you the feeling of joy if you don't remember to give that same amount of effort towards your loved ones. Ask for God's help to keep the balance. There's something more to life than working 60 hours a week.

Sometimes a bad decision in your life can scar you, and some people find it hard to exonerate you. They keep at a respectful distance. Arguments occur that require shifting in thought. It becomes a matter of principle, values and pride. Temper and a hard head go together. It's a tough combo!! Moods that are endearing or infuriating leave you with elation or disappointment. So when you feel down, fight to change it. Don't be in limbo. Life matters. Sheer will is a lifesaver!

Never break the trust of someone you care for. Believe in yourself and God. You will feel so worthwhile by sharing with Him. To all people who come into your life, treat them with tenderness, love and respect because life without an attachment to someone is a lonely place.

Have you ever felt that seeing a certain person always restores you with happy good feelings? That's a quality life! And someone says something to you that goes straight to your heart? Those are the moments that can change your life. So are your priorities in the right place? You'll know because you'll feel it.

Our Father, who art in heaven, hallowed be Thy name. Thy kingdom come. Thy will be done on earth, as it is in heaven. Give us this day our daily bread. And forgive us our debts, as we forgive our debtors. And lead us not into temptation, but deliver us from evil. For Thine is the kingdom, and the power, and the glory, forever. Amen.

OUTLOOK ON LIFE

Dear God,

When Bob's family approached us about buying the Sides home, we thought that was a good idea. I loved living in the house Bob was born in. To me it was an opportunity given with the realities of time. Today I still love it. It is home to me and my family with Bob's spirit and love surrounding me every day.

When you reflect on your life, can you honestly say you're in a better place? I wouldn't trade the "then" for "now." I love the promise of a new day and music that creates a stirring in your heart with wonderful warmth.

Memories are made up of great highs and lows. I've had so many special moments in my life. They stir you and leave you speechless. You'll know that it's God's love taking you out of the trenches into adulthood. He sustains you to keep values in life.

Sometimes what is said is different than what is meant. Be true to yourself, and be true to what matters as you live life. Learn from your mistakes. Pay attention to your surroundings, it's a free pleasure. They are all "quiet company" for you.

Have you ever become friends with someone almost immediately, like in a day, and felt they would live in your heart forever? That's a "wow" moment! Have a great attitude about life. Care about people, and meet new ones. Be happy and lively, accepting what life deals you.

Sometimes we need new horizons and someone to jump start us towards them. It's not a sin to have dreams. Be a person of conscience. Look back on your life and see fun, adventure, and love. Life is not always about what you receive, but also about what you lose and give.

Our Father, who art in heaven, hallowed be Thy name. Thy kingdom come. Thy will be done on earth, as it is in heaven. Give us this day our daily bread. And forgive us our debts, as we forgive our debtors. And lead us not into temptation, but deliver us from evil. For Thine is the kingdom, and the power, and the glory, forever. Amen.

OUTLOOK ON LIFE

Dear God,

In May 2015, God blessed me with another awesome touch of His love. Bobby, a former student, and his father came to my house in Hanover to see me and hug me. When Bobby was in 2nd and 3rd grade, I was his learning disabilities tutor, and he told his father about a teacher who was kind and helpful to him. Now he's married, has three children and lives on the North Shore. He has never forgotten me and my help. I was so touched! I told Bobby to select one of my paintings, and he did! Before they left, his father took a picture of us and the painting. Later he wrote me a letter telling me that he hung the painting in his office. What a loving memory. That's a "wow" moment! Miracles do happen!

If you have commitment and love and trust in yourself, you will be happy. Do you think some people live a life with hardly any responsibilities? We all have something that dominates our lives, be it music, gardening or art. That gives us our salvation. Don't ever lose enthusiasm for something! Have you ever had a day when you felt your problems were lifted and life was not so bad? Your life changes when your thoughts and your needs take a back seat to other people's needs.

A "prayer shawl" is like a hug. I still have Bob's. I believe humor and laughter are healing elements for our lives. It's either cry or laugh, or do both. It all works. Follow your own mind and heart. Feel how lucky you are. We all have the chance to live a life that makes us happy. Don't miss the opportunity. Do you think quarrelling and arguing only leaves us with regrets? So enjoy your life, your partner, your family and friends with a sense of love and purpose. Your eyes and being will reflect your inward gentleness. Share your joys and sadness. It will inspire you to live.

Our Father, who art in heaven, hallowed be Thy name. Thy kingdom come. Thy will be done on earth as it is in heaven. Give us this day our daily bread. And forgive us our debts, as we forgive our debtors. And lead us not into temptation, but deliver us from evil. For Thine is the kingdom and the power, and the glory, forever. Amen.

OUTLOOK ON LIFE

Dear God,

Most people who don't have someone special in their lives believe they're leading busy, rewarding lives with a career as their "Number 1" motivator. Are you one of them? Don't ever get to the point that you almost feel programmed. Life can be more spontaneous, exciting and happy if you mix it up.

Be a good listener. Talk about what's pressing on your mind. Solace comes from a friend, family, and God. You can be happy alone, but it takes liking yourself and laughing at yourself. So are you a giver of comfort to most people? Some good byes are harder than others. They bring tears to your eyes. Lately three of my friends have had to settle their mothers into a care giving place. It's an end of independence, a new chapter in their lives.

Is there something you do every day to make your day more peaceful? For me it's the quiet time I take in the early morning to pray and exercise.

One of the links joining us together is music. One other facet is that we really enjoy each other's company. Can you think of a decision you had to make that changed your life forever? I can after I prayed to God! We all need someone to believe in us. We all have to learn to heal. We all have to build new lives at times after a death, divorce or poor health. Lean on God!

We validate ourselves by our face, our eyes, our thoughts and actions. It makes us the people we are today. Love yourself. Happiness expands when shared. Be interested in other people's lives. Your joy will increase. Savor the opportunity that feeds your being. I was always "Miss Wallflower," very shy. Father sat me down and asked me to work harder on myself and I did. I auditioned for the American Army Band and got the job. I even broadcasted on the radio for thirty minutes once a week in Shanghai. So in spite of flaws, you can blossom and change to become a better person. There's a lot to be said about the word "confidence." It can be good or bad. Take responsibility for what you do. God is in your corner.

Our Father, who art in heaven, hallowed be Thy name. Thy kingdom come. Thy will be done on earth, as it is in heaven. Give us this day our daily bread. And forgive us our debts, as we forgive our debtors. And lead us not into temptation, but deliver us from evil. For Thine is the kingdom, and the power, and the glory, forever. Amen.

OUTLOOK ON LIFE

Dear God,

Today I found a letter from my sister, so I sat down to read it again. She was telling me how much she hated our mother. I think the only way she could deal with it was to "slot-out" that part of her life in Shanghai. I wrote to her to tell her that I understood her action because I wasn't aware that she had been whipped by our mother once. I have never shared this part of my life with you, only with my children. You see, I was beaten constantly by my mother, once seriously when a main vein was cut! I had to run for help to a German doctor who lived near us to stop the bleeding.

My mother, when she was around, hardly spoke to us and never hugged us. I was petrified of her. She called me "Cinderella." I had to do all the chores! If you ever doubt that there is a God, remember my life. I was sent off to boarding school. That was a blessing!! No more beatings!! My teachers and friends all nurtured me. One teacher paid for me to join the Brownies, then Girl Scouts. My godmother took me to church or her home. During the years at boarding school, I never saw my mother. Here again, the head matron was so kind to me.

If you wonder why I have such a "joie de vivre" for God and life, maybe now you will understand. I truly believe that all I endured has made me the kind, caring, loving person I am. I thank God for my "father's" love. He took the time with love and concern for me and my two younger brothers. And without God working in my life, the outcome would have been so different. Thank You, God.

Our Father, who art in heaven, hallowed be Thy name. Thy kingdom come. Thy will be done on earth, as it is in heaven. Give us this day our daily bread. And forgive us our debts, as we forgive our debtors. And lead us not into temptation, but deliver us from evil. For Thine is the kingdom, and the power, and the glory, forever. Amen.

OUTLOOK ON LIFE

Dear God,

Another day with some strong winds blowing the leaves everywhere! It's God's fall dance!

Part of your life is peaceful and happy except for an individual grudge that can last a lifetime! Have you ever met someone who didn't appeal to you? A perfectly wonderful person can feel very alone and frightened within a group. Human nature makes us judge people and things, but ultimately it's God's judgement that matters. Time is relative.

Are you a person who is always thinking ahead? Relax and feel God's love, and make room for Him in your life. You will attain success and contentment. Look for joy in little things. Do you dance and sing around your house? I do! I love being alive. Be a deep, inwardly feeling person instead of an outwardly superficial one. It can change your whole life. Be with people who have big hearts. There's happiness in sharing. We need to know that someone is thinking of us when we're apart.

Sometimes the easy things are the hardest to do. Be generous with praise, have a warm smile. Have you ever felt hopeless in a situation? It's not a good feeling but you must carry on. It's good to do an analysis on your life time to time. It's up to you to choose not to allow hurtful things to happen to you again. You can have everything in life, but without an important center, it will lack meaning.

Do something good each day, something you can be proud of or will last like love. Trust yourself and your wisdom that you've spent half a lifetime accumulating. Be a good listener. To be happy you have to feel loved. It's the most profound feeling to have when we are connected to someone or something. Change happens! God knows you and loves you!

Our Father, who art in heaven, hallowed be Thy name. Thy kingdom come. Thy will be done on earth, as it is in heaven. Give us this day our daily bread. And forgive us our debts, as we forgive our debtors. And lead us not into temptation, but deliver us from evil. For Thine is the kingdom, and the power, and the glory, forever. Amen.

OUTLOOK ON LIFE

Dear God,

It's a different world today! I want to tell each one of you what a treasure you are to me with all your true worth and love. That is what touched my heart. That is what allowed me to write these prayers. I was touched so much. So even at age 86, I still kick up my heels because of you. You are a huge part of my life.

Everyone wants someone to love and to be loved in return. A true friend always feels your happiness or your sadness. That's an "Oscar" moment. Where there is love, there is a smile. Do you have a favorite spot in this world? I love Ogunquit, Maine. Keep your important memories in your mind and in your heart—that's your gift from God. Life is precious.

Do you like the life you have? It's not easy to quell emotions and look on the bright side. Discipline helps. Without the benefit of a close family, you mature and learn self-sufficiency and build a life. Have a kind heart. Extract every drop of you from every hour in a day. Laugh. God will hear you!

Don't worry about bad things that haven't happened yet! Believe that all will be well. Use your eyes, ears and heart. Miracles do happen. Fulfill your life. Nothing is forever if your heart isn't in it. You can't change the past, only the future, and the only place you can change the future is in the present.

People who influence you are the people who believe in you. Inward joy is so important because it radiates outward into your daily life—makes you feel fully alive. Self-worth isn't measured by productivity alone but with ingredients like fun, rest and love with your whole heart. So start your day with a love thought.

Our Father, who art in heaven, hallowed be Thy name. Thy kingdom come. Thy will be done on earth, as it is in heaven. Give us this day our daily bread. And forgive us our debts, as we forgive our debtors. And lead us not into temptation, but deliver us from evil. For Thine is the kingdom, and the power, and the glory, forever. Amen.

OUTLOOK ON LIFE

Dear God,

Most of us have come to terms with our sorrow, be it our own poor health or the poor health of a loved one. We learn our true strength by dealing with it with God's help. New joy is reborn in our hearts in order to be happy. That's not an easy task. It requires honesty and compassion within ourselves. We live by the decisions we make.

Have you ever been excited and worried about something or some person at the same time? In our busy lives we meet with "angels" unaware so many times. Like the members of this choir. A hug or just being there speaks volumes. A friend's love is forever, especially as we go through our ups and downs. If we could only add humor, it would make it so much easier to deal with these times. We all have our own tempo of life, and we all have our own needs. Sharing them with someone makes it a better day. Open your heart. What you store in your heart helps you walk through life a little easier. God will bless a thankful heart.

What are your priorities in life? Warmth and kindness are never wasted. Appreciation for things adds a new dimension to life. Sometimes it takes a major episode in our life to make us thankful. We gain wisdom as we age realizing the joy in simple things with honest laughter and smiles. Whatever you say or do, it affects the one you love. Enjoy being together. People who are loved and happy tend to be less critical of everything.

There's something so invigorating about starting a new chapter in your life. Compromise when you have to because love gives you a safe harbor. Love in the past is just a memory. Love in the here and now brings us happiness. Believe in God. I am so thankful for every day to just wake up. So embrace the whole gift of life from God. Love yourself.

Our Father, who art in heaven, hallowed be Thy name. Thy kingdom come. Thy will be done on earth, as it is in heaven. Give us this day our daily bread. And forgive us our debts, as we forgive our debtors. And lead us not into temptation, but deliver us from evil. For Thine is the kingdom, and the power, and the glory, forever. Amen.

OUTLOOK ON LIFE

Dear God,

Each day as I come to You in prayer I know only You can see and hear into my heart. That is such a comfort! You alone hold the key to what will happen. The world isn't as complicated as it seems, when simple things matter the most!!

Do you think people are destined for one another? I believe that. I know Bob could never be replaced. The most wonderful thing is to love someone and have them love you back. God's love is like that, too. His love makes it possible for us to go on with our life—think about it! It's never too late to change things! You meet someone and realize all the things that have been missing in your life like conversation, truthfulness, endearing qualities and strength from each other. Be at peace with yourself! Walk and exercise. You will feel better and sleep better. It's essential to your well-being!

Do you know someone who is beautiful inside and out? For your own good, you can't be too rich or too beautiful. Have the ability to empathize and the ability to smile through difficult times. Experiences you encounter growing up form you into the person you are. Enjoy being in the moment! Feel a sense of well-being and know your limitations! Compliment other people. Assess your life. Be honest and cut through the clutter!! Enjoy people and feel comfortable with them.

Spontaneity is so important—experience new joy and new adventures. Take courage to do something different! There's more to life than following rules. Life is for living so experience it!!

So don't disappoint yourself, forgive yourself, know who you are. Be good to other people so that when you look at yourself in the mirror, you will like what you see.

Our Father, who art in heaven, hallowed be Thy name. Thy kingdom come. Thy will be done on earth, as it is in heaven. Give us this day our daily bread. And forgive us our debts, as we forgive our debtors. And lead us not into temptation, but deliver us from evil. For Thine is the kingdom, and the power, and the glory, forever. Amen.

OUTLOOK ON LIFE

Dear God,

As we age, we become more nostalgic about places and people. We can't change the past, only the future. Have your ever felt that time stood still in this ever-changing world? Have you thought you could be in the past or present? Life is full of surprises, some pleasant and some not so. The course of our lives can change so quickly if something is said or not said. Sometimes we feel one thing and say another. We worry about following the rules rather than taking chances.

We should use more heart and less brain. To see our children juggling work and family and responsibilities is a blessing. Home—it's a magical word! It means family, friends, people, happiness, love and memories. We all need to live in the world as it is, not as it was. Email is fine, but I still write longhand notes. We should make sure we don't make the same monumental mistake twice by learning a lesson about life and having a chance to correct it. Take charge of events before they take charge of you.

Have character, humor, smile and be a truthful person who is nice to know. Everyone needs a love of a lifetime. It completes us as a whole person because we can be self-sacrificing, frightened, and less thoughtful, depending on how we were brought up. Make some alone time for getting to know yourself better. Feel God's love surrounding you. Put a wonderful thought in your mind that makes you smile. Keep this agenda going and God will smile.

Our Father, who art in heaven, hallowed be Thy name. Thy kingdom come. Thy will be done on earth, as it is in heaven.

Give us this day our daily bread. And forgive us our debts, as we forgive our debtors. And lead us not into temptation, but deliver us from evil. For Thine is the kingdom, and the power, and the glory, forever. Amen.

OUTLOOK ON LIFE

Dear God,

When you always rely on a person, the day will come when you have to face facts that they will leave. It's not easy. Even though time passes I'm brutally sentimental, and I relied so much on Bob. A loving person sends out a message with their eyes and their voice. The course you set in life doesn't always work out the way you planned. It takes a long time to get over missing someone. It's a heartache.

With God you realize that true love is forever. True love changes your world, and you learn that with true love you can cope with sorrow. You never know how people will react to upsetting news. We have many choices in life, and they change constantly. Sometimes there is no all right or all wrong way as long as you try. Sometimes old resentments come rolling in to boil again, and if you can't forget that past, it's not possible to accept it and move on.

Do you only have two speeds, stop or go? Have ambition, excitement, energy, and the realization that your life is blessed. Do you plan every aspect of your day because your mind just won't shut off? Trust your own judgment. Enjoy the ride if you're content in your personal life or challenged in your professional life.

You need to be happy even if you have a habitual routine you live by. Open your mind to possibilities. We're not perfect people. Step back and take an honest look at your life and understand it. Notice the kind faces around you. Have you ever met someone you really didn't care for or trust? I have. It's a rude awakening!! You can't lose what you never had in the first place.

Our Father, who art in heaven, hallowed be Thy name. Thy kingdom come. Thy will be done on earth, as it is in heaven. Give us this day our daily bread. And forgive us our debts, as we forgive our debtors. And lead us not into temptation, but deliver us from evil. For Thine is the kingdom, and the power, and the glory, forever. Amen.

OUTLOOK ON LIFE

Dear God,

The sky is clear and the sun is bright, a perfect spring day! If you walk the beach, listen to the chirping seagulls and smell the scent of wind and sea. There's something special and mystical about being on the water at dawn watching the day break. It really renews your spirit!

Live according to your values. You are responsible for your own health. Mother yourself! Unmet needs create stress, so voice your needs and face your emotions. God and friends will help.

In some instances you feel awful even though your intentions were good! Tell people what they mean to you in your life and how much you care. It's a funny thing about truth. It always comes out. We have to prioritize as a couple because it creates togetherness.

Don't let other people dictate how you live. Sometimes problems become an opportunity because life is subject to change without notice. To be alone and not have someone special in your life to love and care for is sad!!

Facial expressions tell a story; it's a nuance of our language. To be happy you have to feel and love people who inspire you. Generally do what's true and right. Be confident and caring. Thank God for being by your side and always there to give us new strength. Trust Him. Age is wisdom! We should all buy a gift to ourselves at some time. Be kind and good-hearted.

Our Father, who art in heaven, hallowed be Thy name. Thy kingdom come. Thy will be done on earth, as it is in heaven.

Give us this day our daily bread. And forgive us our debts, as we forgive our debtors. And lead us not into temptation, but deliver us from evil. For Thine is the kingdom, and the power, and the glory, forever. Amen.

OUTLOOK ON LIFE

Dear God,

Life has a beginning, middle and end, a gift from God. No matter the age we live as our health allows us to—free, loved, and active. I enjoy watching people and hearing music. It makes us happy to walk or dance. It is sweet happiness. Life is good. Do you have a face that lives in its smiles? Have exuberance for something each day. Be aware of other people's needs. Single-mindedness isn't always a good quality because if your focus is on one thing you don't pay attention to what else is being spoken or done.

Have a wicked sense of humor and down to earth practicality. Do you wonder about the roads not taken? Know what you want and go for it. Choose the path you want to follow. Unfortunately time doesn't make it easy to stay on course. A person can get used to anything, given enough time.

Believe in God and the power of prayer. Enjoy simple things that money can't buy. Some people don't change, they just get older. Work hard, but take time to have fun and pleasure, too. Savor it! Have you ever felt homesick? Or experienced the idea of missing someone you love, your home, or your family? It's so great when you can trust a person. Meeting a friend for lunch is just the best antidote for a terrible day!

Be passionate about life instead of just drifting. You have to land sometime. Has your heart ever swelled with emotions that bring tears to your eyes? Mine has, so many times on humorous occasions. Be reflective on the content of your life when walking. There is a thrill in expecting the unexpected. A good kind of crazy!!

Our Father, who art in heaven, hallowed be Thy name. Thy kingdom come. Thy will be done on earth, as it is in heaven. Give us this day our daily bread. And forgive us our debts, as we forgive our debtors. And lead us not into temptation, but deliver us from evil. For Thine is the kingdom, and the power, and the glory, forever. Amen.

OUTLOOK ON LIFE

Dear God,

Sometimes it's hard to be brave and gutsy. I have learned that simple truths and values can help you avoid many heartaches. I have also learned that one of the greatest comforts in life is the bond of love and friendship. Have you ever felt emotional about someone? It's a totally different feeling when you realize how precious everything is about that person in your life. Train your mind to learn something new all the time.

Listening, really listening, is different than just hearing. Sometimes a bad thing turns into a different opportunity that leaves you grateful and reassured. Compliment someone every day with sincerity. Be full of hope because God alone knows your whole life. Rescue comes in the most unexpected moment. Love always finds a way. When you have happiness in your life, share it. Your face tells a person the decision you're making if you're happy with it or not. Thank God for it. Life couldn't get much better.

Do you have a restful place the rest of the world can't intrude? We always regret what we don't do rarely what we do. Stop blaming yourself for past mistakes. In my warmth of memories I feel it's so great to greet a new day. It's a gift from God and to know that Bob's love and care are by my side is a happiness within my heart. Bond with people who create a feeling of love that's spoken with their whole body. Take a deep breath. Practice mindful thinking about what you can control and push away what you can't. Believe in God's love.

Our Father, who art in heaven, hallowed be Thy name. Thy kingdom come. Thy will be done on earth, as it is in heaven.

Give us this day our daily bread. And forgive us our debts, as we forgive our debtors. And lead us not into temptation, but deliver us from evil. For Thine is the kingdom, and the power, and the glory, forever. Amen.

OUTLOOK ON LIFE

Dear God,

Being independent and responsible requires guidance and direction in whatever we undertake to do. The choices are ours to bring us to a plateau of living our life. It's difficult to break a habit, to be brave and gutsy in unfamiliar territory. Do you show a different face to different people? Think about tomorrow instead of today because today keeps being "just today!!"

Say "yes" or "no;" "maybe" is so indecisive! Bond with people who create love and affection. Everyone has a different sense of right and wrong, it's a subjective thing. However, intellect deals with facts, whereas emotions are variable. Life is a series of choices. Action and circumstance often are the result of other peoples' choice. Believe in yourself for we all have pitfalls to overcome. God's love will see you through the trying times. Feel comfortable in your own skin. Living through a war, there were days when I felt life was worthless. Prayer worked magic!

Do you believe that faith can move mountains? There are three words: yours, mine and ours. Ours is the best!! So talk about what is bothering you, then you don't get overwhelmed.

Things change and so do people. Tackle something that absorbs you, and put passion and strength in your effort. It will take you into a neutral zone where your "got-to-do" list fades in importance. If you're lucky enough to find joy and happiness in life, hold onto it, and nurture it like some gorgeous flower. Do you have a celebration meal for a great happy moment? Have a tempo in life—it's so far reaching! Love God.

Our Father, who art in heaven, hallowed be Thy name. Thy kingdom come. Thy will be done on earth, as it is in heaven. Give us this day our daily bread. And forgive us our debts, as we forgive our debtors. And lead us not into temptation, but deliver us from evil. For Thine is the kingdom, and the power, and the glory, forever. Amen.

OUTLOOK ON LIFE

Dear God,

In relationships we sometimes forget how important it is to consider how others feel and what they think about situations. It's so easy to get huffy within an exchange of verbal conversation and hurt feelings. Life is too short to let it remain that way. Work it out. It happens to all of us! In contrast, have you ever had goose bumps over some good news or happening? That's a great moment of the heart!

What is your talent? Is it athletic, academic, artistic, or musical, or do you have an infectious smile that can brighten any room? It seems so unfair when a mother puts so much effort into rearing her child and that result is the total opposite of her hopes. It happens. Do good things come to people who wait with patience? Showing kindness to a person always gets repaid by that person being kind to someone else.

Love your family and friends every day if you want a happy life. Think about your choices. Do you take chances in your life? Sometimes the outcomes are good. Or, do you have a priority list you work from every day? I hope you love where you live. I do. It's where I want to be.

It's nice to be proud of our children; however, they extract some values from us so we have to be sure of our messages to them. In some situations even though we try our best there's nothing we can do to change it. Time flies even when you're NOT having fun so enjoy every day. One person in your life can make such a difference. Have an honest attitude. Reaffirm what is important to you. We're all born with an interest or talent that some go on to nurture. Embrace your uniqueness. It will give you joy. God loves you.

Our Father, who art in heaven, hallowed be Thy name. Thy kingdom come. Thy will be done on earth, as it is in heaven. Give us this day our daily bread. And forgive us our debts, as we forgive our debtors. And lead us not into temptation, but deliver us from evil. For Thine is the kingdom, and the power, and the glory, forever. Amen.

OUTLOOK ON LIFE

Dear God,

Some people who haven't gone through a horrific trauma in life can't fully understand and appreciate every day and feel how precious it is. Bob was a gift to my life!

Have you ever dreaded the day when you had some bad news to convey to someone or to family? It happens to most of us. Our needs are a daily thing. Lean on God. He hears you.

Do you fear change? I know I surprised myself by coming to America! So-o-o many changes. Humor helped me through many awkward situations.

Do you have rationale in your thinking? Be truthful! For me it was so wonderful to have someone who wanted to take care of me and embrace me in love forever. It was a miracle! My emotional, inward strengths were enhanced by appreciation, moment to moment, by kindness, and by thoughtfulness.

I love people! Have a big heart and be willing to compromise. Be gentle to yourself. Enjoy each day. Be dependable. Express your true feelings. It avoids stress dealing with a problem. Are your good deeds done for "Show and Tell" or are they from your heart? Remember, God sees into your heart.

So enjoy music, dance, exercise, golf, and boat rides. Take time for a walk. You'll feel so much happier. Give love and receive it. Smile. Life is good, in spite of some bad times. Flowers are like soul food for the heart, and God is the answer to every prayer. Look for joy in little things. Nothing is worth a quarrel. We all have dreams for the future. Try to worry about things one at a time. It's rewarding to hear how you influenced someone in life. So it's important to know who you are and where you're going. Do it with a vision of love because God is love.

Our Father, who art in heaven, hallowed be Thy name. Thy kingdom come. Thy will be done on earth, as it is in heaven. Give us this day our daily bread. And forgive us our debts, as we forgive our debtors. And lead us not into temptation, but deliver us from evil. For Thine is the kingdom, and the power, and the glory, forever. Amen.

OUTLOOK ON LIFE

Dear God,

I find you can't run away from reality. What happened to you in the past shapes you into who you are today. Are you happy with your life? Try with confidence to achieve success and feel rock solid every day even if you have to use your safety valve. Some things are non-negotiable even in a crisis. Do you think that to succeed in business you have to say and do things with some bravado?

Honesty and humor can make your day. Looking inwardly at yourself, can you say that you're a different person now than you were before? God, You alone know the way that I must go. I'm always glad to feel Your hand for a fresh, new day with love. As parents we wing it, doing things in a different way not according to a plan. It's difficult with no easy answers at times.

Do we get second chances? I'd say that sometimes we do. We get a second chance with actions and words that count. That's a blessing from God. Put yourself in someone else's shoes to feel and solve a problem. It's so healing. Failing in new endeavors or difficult ones shouldn't stop you from trying. It's worth it.

Friends are always relevant to your life. Best friends are a gold mine. Childhood friends are irreplaceable. When someone we love is in pain, we suffer right along with them. When you met your sweetheart did you think that was a date with destiny? And did circumstances verify it for you? Whenever one of the children or I find a penny, we feel Bob. There is love and there is deep heart love you can feel for a person. Deep heart love is different. It's so easy to mentally rewrite past mistakes after the fact. Facing the truth is the difficult part. The decisions we make are a lesson learned. Being happy is the end result fulfilled.

Our Father, who art in heaven, hallowed be Thy name. Thy kingdom come. Thy will be done on earth, as it is in heaven. Give us this day our daily bread. And forgive us our debts, as we forgive our debtors. And lead us not into temptation, but deliver us from evil. For Thine is the kingdom, and the power, and the glory, forever. Amen.

OUTLOOK ON LIFE

Dear God,

Time after time You forgive us for our mistakes and love each one of us totally. To have that in our lives is a gift forever. When something awesome happens in your life and you're filled with happiness, do you feel like an angel is sitting on your shoulder? Know who you are and love yourself. Put down roots, be a life partner and savor the joy of life. Hold on to what is sacred to you. Try to have a sunny disposition with spirit.

I come from a generation when mothers stayed home to care for their children. In reflection I'm glad I did because when I started to work, I never stopped until retirement. Are you a person who cuts to the chase? Who speaks out in any situation? Or do you have difficulty with that and consequently say nothing or make a slight comment? Either way takes finesse verbally and that doesn't necessarily produce results. Take time to be quiet and think about your concerns in life. Focus on love and friendships. Try new things. Look people in the eye!

Have you ever thought about the word "home?" It's a place you love and feel safe in, a place that fits you best and is filled with memories and family. Live each day to the best of your ability. Everyone has something happen in their lives that puts God's strength into dealing with it so you can move forward. Thank You, God.

In a crowd of people you can still feel alone if there is no love amongst them for you. Do you think there is a time and a place for everything? Things do happen and you feel guided by fate. Listen to your heart. Have a sense of self-acceptance that you're not perfect. Be humble. It's a good thing. Be happy to be alive.

Getting old together doesn't always work out that way. Feel love and happiness. God wants you to know what makes the world go 'round.

Our Father, who art in heaven, hallowed be Thy name. Thy kingdom come. Thy will be done on earth, as it is in heaven. Give us this day our daily bread. And forgive us our debts, as we forgive our debtors. And lead us not into temptation, but deliver us from evil. For Thine is the kingdom, and the power, and the glory, forever. Amen.

OUTLOOK ON LIFE

Dear God,

Some people have professional responsibilities plus personal ones that both need effort and caring. Sometimes you feel like you're stepping on firm ground and other times you feel like you're stepping on quick sand with enough drama to last a lifetime.

Do you think the world is divided into three roads and you happen to walk the middle road? We all need composure, flexibility, and acceptance to turn the tide of emotion. Make the most of your life, face decisions, tackle problems, and be true to yourself. We all face love and loss. Lives can be rebuilt.

Impulsiveness is exhilarating, but also exhausting!! We all have something that's therapeutic that we do when we're upset. It could be gardening, saying a prayer, or going to a particular place, or just being quiet. Do you know someone who has such a busy life that evolves only around themselves? Their values are totally different from yours.

Have you even felt disowned by your mother? I have. My brothers said the same thing after we got to America. Thank God for our father who gave us love and hugs, and Baby-Amah and other people who filled in for a mother who wasn't there for us. She was only there in her own life for herself. I'm sure it's one of the reasons I'm so affectionate. One good thing we learned was responsibility. At 16 I had to work and build my own wardrobe. I was on my own for everything. Thank You, God, for giving me another chance with my life to be alive and happy. That is so awesome!

316

Be sensitive to other people's feelings. Try to make a person feel good. Be involved in your own life. Make it different if it needs to be. Be loyal and tender to all. Make decisions in the crossroads in life that give you peace and joy and pleasure in everything. God wants you to have that life. At 86 I'm here! Yeah!

Our Father, who art in heaven, hallowed be Thy name. Thy kingdom come. Thy will be done on earth, as it is in heaven. Give us this day our daily bread. And forgive us our debts, as we forgive our debtors. And lead us not into temptation, but deliver us from evil. For Thine is the kingdom, and the power, and the glory, forever. Amen.

OUTLOOK ON LIFE

Dear God,

Isn't it beautiful to see the stars and moon playing between the clouds? It's another gift from You. It's so easy to find things that make you happy. Be spontaneous instead of predictable! Know how to love other people. When you're personally involved with someone, your time is no longer your own. Half the battle in life is knowing what works for you.

We all do some things because we convince ourselves it's the right thing to do. As a parent, we can be the right or wrong compass for our children. Be honest with yourself. Know your strengths and weaknesses. Work on the weak ones. You'll be pleasantly surprised at the results. We are blessed to be around to see our grown children hug each other. Thank You, God.

Some things that happen within a passage of time you can never forget. Be sure you're still not living the problem. Keep commitments to good things, and do them with love, not out of duty. Relationships are keepers. Don't let age constrict your mind from doing fun things. Appreciate what you have learned in life, and share it with people. This is a wonderful life. Give love and also receive it. Smile for the love of your family and friends. Own grace and beauty and all of it will radiate out of you. It's God's gift to you.

Enjoy each day. How you spend your time during a difficult time really counts. It takes strength to hold on to inner passion to make life worthwhile. Bob was always there to comfort me with kindness. I see that same kindness in my daughters and that touches my heart. We need God. He truly opens our being to what works for us. Have you ever felt God's presence in your life? His love is like a cuddly blanket.

Our Father, who art in heaven, hallowed be Thy name. Thy kingdom come. Thy will be done on earth, as it is in heaven. Give us this day our daily bread. And forgive us our debts, as we forgive our debtors. And lead us not into temptation, but deliver us from evil. For Thine is the kingdom, and the power, and the glory, forever. Amen.

OUTLOOK ON LIFE

Dear God,

Thank You for letting me continue to live in my home without Bob. It's a huge, happy comfort for me. I feel his spirt and love. That's one of the things he left me. Make every day a quality day in your life. You'll feel the difference. You will feel inner joy. Never let go of your hopes and dreams. Not everything is solved by a pill or wine. Love and togetherness are so important.

Have you ever had a mixture of emotions when you're anxious and happy simultaneously? Or, have you tried to please everyone and ended up pleasing no one? Our values come out of what human conditions we live through. Don't you love that moment when you feel like your joyful feet are hardly touching the ground? Savor that moment. Never put your friendships in jeopardy, no matter how wide your friendship circle is. It's a blessing to have loved ones to enjoy. It's a dimension straight from the heart. Have a sense of responsibility in life. It begins with you! We need joy and fruitful relationships. We need God for strength and comfort to deal with our lives.

What is your tempo in life? As we age, we learn that contentment and simple honesties are a great comfort. Feel loved. Feel kindness and thoughtfulness in your whole being. That's a good life! With the loss of someone you love, you have to dig deeply within your psyche to figure out how to forge a new life. We all have our own internal compass. Happiness needs nothing but itself. It multiplies easily. Realize God's love in your life. What does your body language say to the world? I hope it reflects love.

Our Father, who art in heaven, hallowed be Thy name. Thy kingdom come. Thy will be done on earth, as it is in heaven.

Give us this day our daily bread. And forgive us our debts, as we forgive our debtors. And lead us not into temptation, but deliver us from evil. For Thine is the kingdom, and the power, and the glory, forever. Amen.